FIVE HUNDRED 45s

FIVE HUNDRED 45s

A GRAPHIC HISTORY OF THE SEVEN-INCH RECORD

SPENCER DRATE AND JUDITH SALAVETZ

COLLINS DESIGN
An Imprint of HarperCollins Publishers

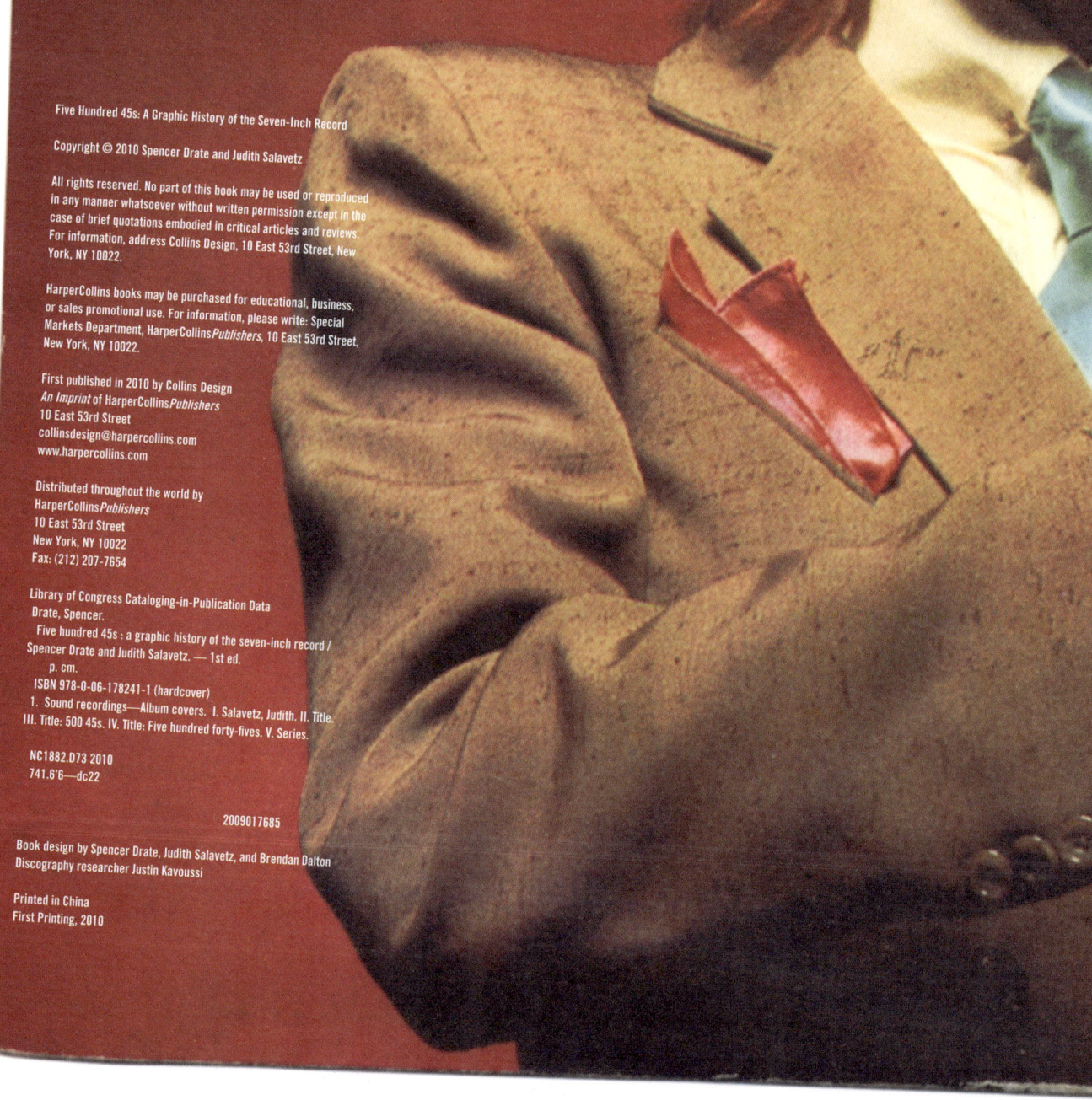

Five Hundred 45s: A Graphic History of the Seven-Inch Record

Copyright © 2010 Spencer Drate and Judith Salavetz

All rights reserved. No part of this book may be used or reproduced in any manner whatsoever without written permission except in the case of brief quotations embodied in critical articles and reviews. For information, address Collins Design, 10 East 53rd Street, New York, NY 10022.

HarperCollins books may be purchased for educational, business, or sales promotional use. For information, please write: Special Markets Department, HarperCollins*Publishers*, 10 East 53rd Street, New York, NY 10022.

First published in 2010 by Collins Design
An Imprint of HarperCollins*Publishers*
10 East 53rd Street
collinsdesign@harpercollins.com
www.harpercollins.com

Distributed throughout the world by
HarperCollins*Publishers*
10 East 53rd Street
New York, NY 10022
Fax: (212) 207-7654

Library of Congress Cataloging-in-Publication Data
Drate, Spencer.
  Five hundred 45s : a graphic history of the seven-inch record / Spencer Drate and Judith Salavetz. — 1st ed.
    p. cm.
  ISBN 978-0-06-178241-1 (hardcover)
  1. Sound recordings—Album covers. I. Salavetz, Judith. II. Title. III. Title: 500 45s. IV. Title: Five hundred forty-fives. V. Series.

NC1882.D73 2010
741.6'6—dc22

2009017685

Book design by Spencer Drate, Judith Salavetz, and Brendan Dalton
Discography researcher Justin Kavoussi

Printed in China
First Printing, 2010

FOREWORD
INTRODUCTION: 45 REVOLUTIONS PER MILLENNIUM — 6

— 8

WONDERBREAD, HOT DOGS, FROSTED FLAKES, AND ELVIS

SINGLES GOING STEADY: THE WORK OF JEFF KLEINSMITH — 80

— 156

A BRIEF, BIASED, AND LIKELY BULLSH*T HISTORY OF THE PUNK SEVEN-INCH 45 RPM RECORD — 242

FIFTEEN BUCKS FOR "FUCKHEAD"

ON LETTERPRESS AND RECORD SLEEVES — 330

— 398

DISCOGRAPHY
ACKNOWLEDGMENTS — 461

— 479

FOREWORD

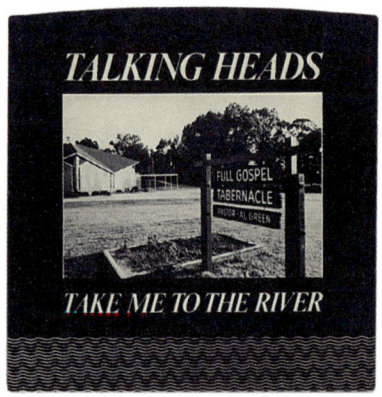  

I was a kid when my dad gave me my very first 45 record—"Hound Dog" by Elvis Presley—and it completely rocked my world. I loved listening to the song over and over, but more than the sound, it was the look of the sleeve that really got me. Black and white, highly graphic, with an outrageous photograph of Elvis and a basset hound wearing a miniature top hat—the perfectly small 7-inch square had so much character, I was totally wild about it! My love and enthusiasm for that single catapulted me into a lifelong addiction to 45 records. I bought more and more—low cost being one of their great qualities—and as my collection grew, I found that while some sleeves, like "Hound Dog," were photographic, others featured beautiful art and illustrations or striking typography. Each aesthetically appealing in its own way, these sleeves were 7-inch canvases on which musicians painted their public image.

Not only did I love to collect 45s, but these visual gems influenced my career as well: I wound up being a designer and art director of music packaging—album covers and single sleeves—and often worked with fellow designer and 45-lover Judith Salavetz. Our shared love of single sleeves led us to realize that bookstores, though full of books on album and CD design, lacked any publication that showcased all the awesome designs of 45s. Something had to be done. So in 2002, Judith and I wrote *45 RPM: A Visual History of the Seven-Inch Record*—a great book with many amazing sleeves—but we were left unsatisfied. There were so many gorgeous sleeves that we couldn't include in the first book. That is why we had to make *Five Hundred 45s*. This treasure trove of 7-inch sleeves is bigger and better, and includes a stunning gallery of 500 unique 45 record sleeves. 45s rock!

SPENCER DRATE

The 45 became a very special medium in the pop music world. It allowed for the instant gratification of listening to a single track of music (or maybe two tracks, since many B-sides became equally popular or even more so than the A-side). And this gratification was for everyman, particularly adolescents. For many younger purchasers, 45s were a relatively cheap extravagance. For the popular tunes, the process was: hear it on the radio or watch the newest hot artist/group on *Bandstand* or on *The Ed Sullivan Show*. Then run down to the record store as soon as it opened or on the way home from school and buy it for 49 cents, or 59 cents, or even 69 cents. But just buy it because you had to have it.

I always thought the 45 record buying process was great fun. Part of the fun came from the aesthetics, which added greatly to the excitement generated from the emotional response to listening to the music (usually over and over again, ad infinitum). The records themselves were fun to look at. The labels had exotic names such as Chess, Coral, Atlantic, Roulette, SMASH, and so many others, including a strange one showing a curious spaniel looking into an old victrola speaker. The label colors and fonts tended to be exotic, strong, bright colors and incorporated all kinds of crazy designs and icons. As an artist learning the ropes of design, I thought the 45 album sleeve was the icing on the cake. As 45s became the vehicle for instant stardom, the sleeve design let you see the artist, often for the very first time. There wasn't nearly the variety of media that exists today to see the artists, many of whom were obscure until they emerged quickly from hype and frequent play on radio shows. The sleeve images formed the first impression, and many of these impressions have stuck with 45 buyers like me for many years since.

Along with Spencer, I have designed many LP albums and CD covers, ever since 45s started to fade as the record purchase of choice. Most are more complex artistically, and some are more subtle than the best 45 sleeves. But the 45 sleeves still retain their startling impact as the visual introduction to the artist. These records provided a special emotional package of music with label and sleeve imagery. Spencer and I are very gratified to bring the range of sleeve design into focus in the pages of this book.

JUDITH SALAVETZ

AS 45s BECAME THE VEHICLE FOR INSTANT STARDOM, THE SLEEVE DESIGN LET YOU SEE THE ARTIST, OFTEN FOR THE VERY FIRST TIME.

INTRODUCTION
45 REVOLUTIONS PER MILLENNIUM

I remember the day the 45 seduced my discographic heart, my phonographic soul. I was eleven, walked into Vogel's Record Shop on Flatbush Avenue in Brooklyn, and bought four records, thus beginning a lifetime of obsession, accumulation, and fascination. Those first four 45s—the seeds of my ever-growing collection—were Sheb Wooley's "The Purple People Eater," Conway Twitty's "It's Only Make Believe," Tommy Edwards' "It's All in the Game," and a version of "To Know Him Is To Love Him" performed by Cathy Carr, which I bought thinking it was the Teddy Bears' version, which was on the Billboard Top 100 chart at that time. These 45s epitomized novelty and romance—two things I've always been about—especially when they come in small packages. They had an A and a B side, were highly portable, and were collectable souvenirs of the songs' experiences, as much fun to flip through and file and caress (do accompany me to the Allentown, Pennsylvania, 45 flea market sometime) as letting its song fly into the air. Ownership of music—the commoditization of performance—is akin to joining the fan club of the record at hand, even now, on the download, when the pleasure of an artifact is seeing the title and a cover touch screen by which there is a thrill of belonging.

The size of the 7-inch 45 made it easy to possess, following in evolution from the bulky 10-inch 78 rpm shellac discs that preceded it on Edison's family tree (though he was more of a cylinder man). The previous storage medium had been heavy, prone to breakage, and amenable to the scratch of surface noise. Part of the charm perhaps, but certainly not one geared to the jet-streamed fifties, on the cusp of auto tailfins and high fidelity.

On March 31, 1949, RCA Victor—a record company that also provided players, a marketing sleight-of-hand combining both hardware and software—debuted their "new 45 system... everything from a bebop bash to a minuet"—in a variety of colored vinyl, including black (popular), classical (red), country and western (green), and rhythm and blues (cerise, better known as orange). Rock and roll had yet to be invented.

Rock and roll was awaiting the 45. More serious music lovers, of jazz or classical, even left over "pops" from the big bands, were taken with Columbia's format update, the $33\frac{1}{3}$ rpm long-playing album. Which left the newly minted teenager class, with their sock hops and ducktails and juvenile delinquents, to make full use of the smaller-but-faster format, amid a rise of independent record companies who saw opportunity in regional genre—blues, rockabilly, gospel—along with a cheap way of pressing, and more important, distributing 45s so they were easier to get around, and around, and around.

For the next forty-some years, until the compact disc blurred the boundaries of album and single (making them the same size, part of the record company's cabal to maximize profits by getting the public to buy the album, not their favorite slice of pop pizza), the 45 was the dominant purveyor of individual song, engaged in a symbiotic tug-of-war with the 33⅓ "album" that saw each urge the other on. This relationship was not always so incestuous; the 45 and the 33⅓ were designed to duel to the death. Both formats, from spindle size to rotational, were purposely incompatible. RCA had the large hole, and could fit the accepted length of a song—itself a byproduct of Edison's ability to put up to five minutes of playing time on a side—in its furrows. The 33⅓ record was about as low an orbital speed as you could go and still retain fidelity; RCA upped the rpm and went for the single. Columbia opted for the album. By 1951 each had seen that resistance to the other was useless and started making records in both configurations, during the medieval years before stereo and quad, cassette and eight-track, and our digital domain—all of 'em needing a song and a sleeve. Like the heart one wears upon it, the illustration provided by a record's jacket sets the tone, creates the mood, pins the up, allows the visuals to amplify, as a good speaker will, the song. Protects and projects.

Without the relatively big 12-inch canvas of a long-playing record, sometimes the 45 sleeve has taken a backseat in design. Yet even in smaller scale, as each new musical generation fashions its own accessories, accompanied by ever-changing fonts and hair lengths; in millisecond delay, the covers echo the cultural changes wrought. The third of a century in which the 45 held sway in the marketplace was the last pre-mass computational era, and the single, a telling word that contains its own song, was the equivalent of hypertext, a semaphore of soundtrack. Disposable, transportable, you could grab a handful and become your own disc jockey. Tack the sleeve on the wall, because that's the way you look at that particular shard of self-expression. And it looks back at you.

Or so we like to think. Actually, a travel through time, as this book collates, provokes nothing less than wonder at cult signifiers and groupthink. The sweep of the pompadour on a heavy-lidded fifties rockabilly rebel; the cut

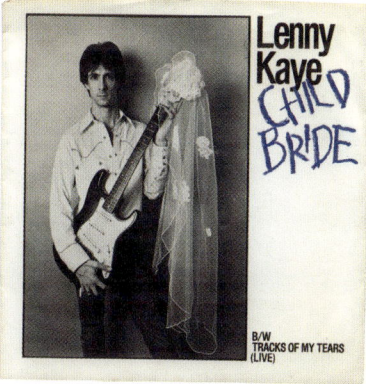

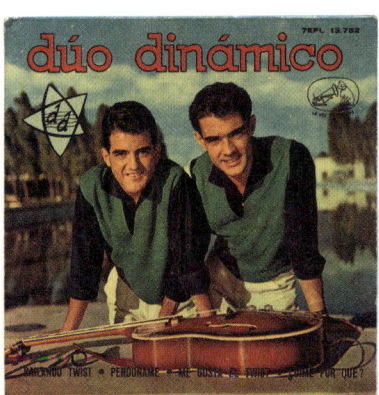

of a Nehru suit on the mid-sixties psychedelic guitarist; a ripped, slashed, and safety-pinned punk confrontational from the year when two sevens clashed; each with its distinctive color scheme, pastel to Day-Glo to black-is-black. In spectrum they parade past, shooting stars blipped across the heavens of one-shot glory to Elvisian giants bestriding the earth, their sleeves suffused with the knowledge that they have entered the time frame. The moment they have been waiting for.

There are moments in the history of the 45 that seem particularly favorable to visual creativity. In Europe, all singles came in picture sleeves, and when this began to translate to the English Invasion, both the Beatles and Stones, as well as the Yardbirds (my favorite), begat collectibles galore. The seventies punk and later hardcore explosion also yielded memorable graphophonica, a do-it-yourself aesthetic that provided the last great gasp of 45 art before the CD single became its own contradiction. There was a renaissance in the 1990s when the format seemed to signify authenticity. That there is an abiding interest in the solitary song is now the driving force behind the new emphasis on singles, the individual track on the download, remixes not included.

A single stands alone. An album, by its very definition, relies on segue and assemblage, the emphasis on the artisan. But in a single, the song takes precedence. Though artistic context may be generated over the chronological accumulation of a "career," the listening experience has a beginning and an end, when the needle runs out of track. All that comes between is finite. Appreciated on its own terms, a single—like our individual lifespan—is a world unto itself.

It follows that its sleeve, the dress shirt put on for a special occasion, a party, perhaps, or a grand ball, is an adornment chosen with care. We like to make a good first impression. For a single, having a picture sleeve is dress-up. Most 45s garb themselves in workaday clothes, the undergarment of a plain brown or white wrapper. But at a singles bar, you need to stand out, so you can find someone to buy you a drink, take you home, and be your partner—in the case of the 45, the matchmaking of listener and song.

I must admit, I'm a profligate disco-izer, sometimes going home with several at one time (whoooee!) and a sucker for something a bit out of the *ordinaire*: see "Dúo Dinámico" and "Bed Spring Motel" on the opposite page.

So here I am in Allentown, flipping through the stacks, occasionally extracting a disc from the wrapper to inspect its condition, thinking of how it fits into the overall accumulation of sound and fury that is spread out in front of me, divided by musical type, time, and tenacity. How did this record get to here, from initial thought-up chord to press-record to pressing plant to a random pile trucked in from the Midwest, to wind up with me?

I look at the sleeve.

The faces—human, type—stare out at me. They're about to start singing.

Give 'em a whirl.

LENNY KAYE

LIKE THE HEART
ONE WEARS UPON IT, THE
ILLUSTRATION
PROVIDED BY A
RECORD'S JACKET
SETS THE TONE, CREATES THE MOOD.

LOVE ON A FARMBOY'S WAGES

XTC

CALEXICO

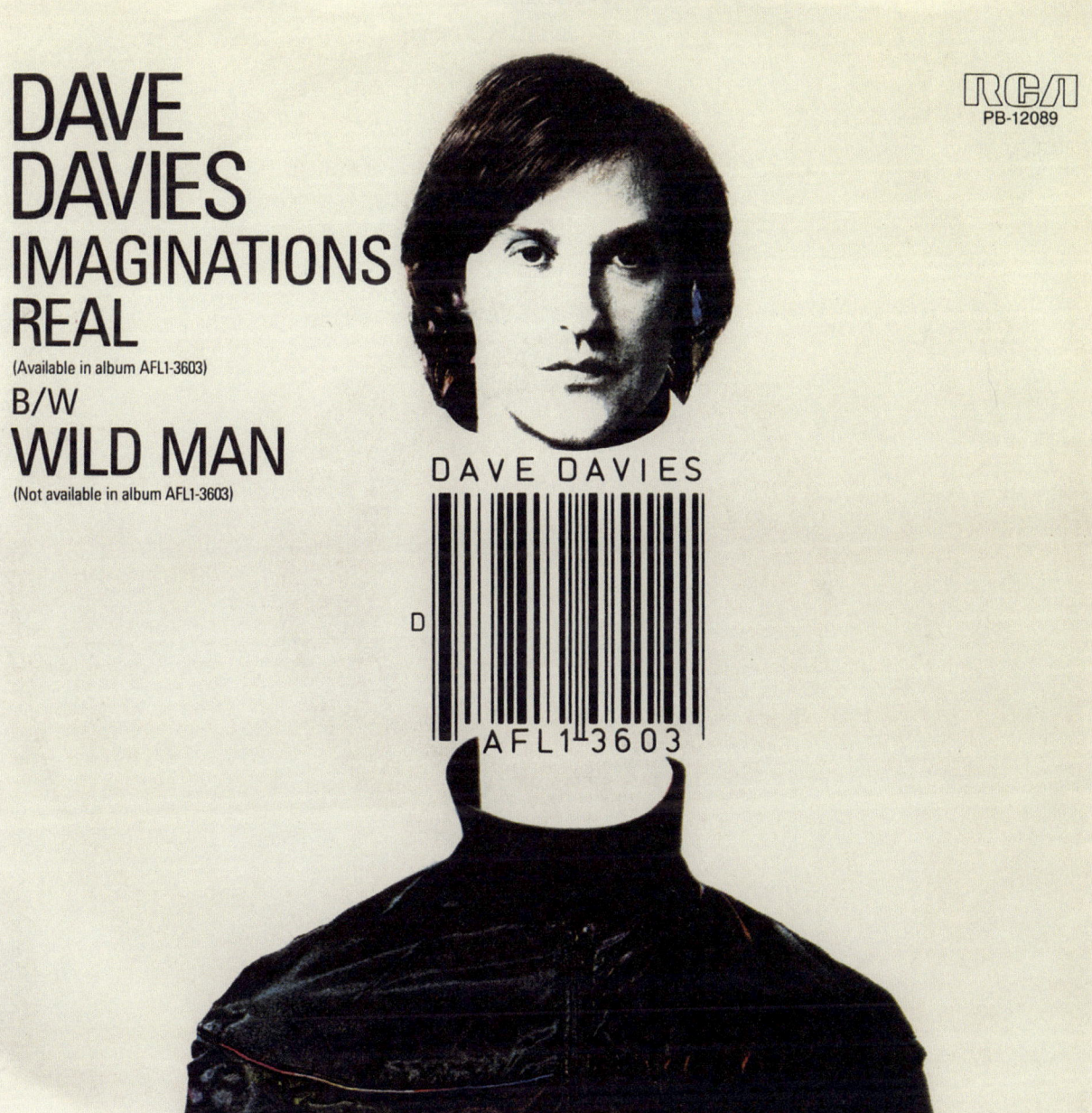

B-2507

I'VE HEARD THAT SONG BEFORE
I HAD THE CRAZIEST DREAM
I DON'T WANT TO WALK WITHOUT YOU
SKYLARK

HARRY JAMES
AND HIS ORCHESTRA FEATURING
HELEN FORREST

vertigo
driver #43

THE BEATLES

I SAW HER STANDING THERE
I WANT TO HOLD YOUR HAND

5112

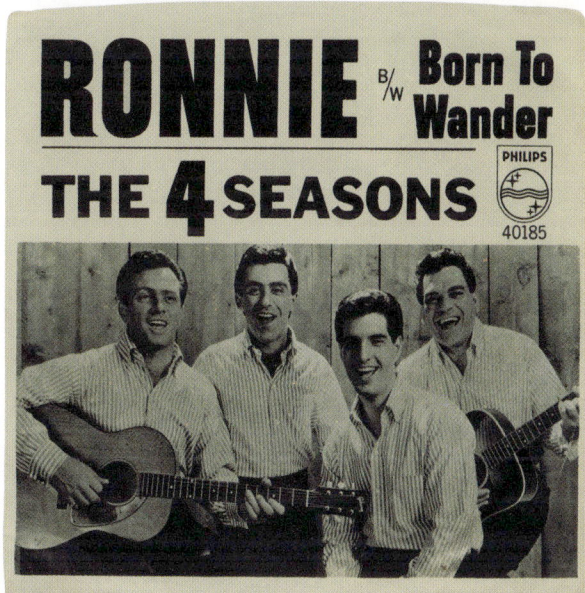

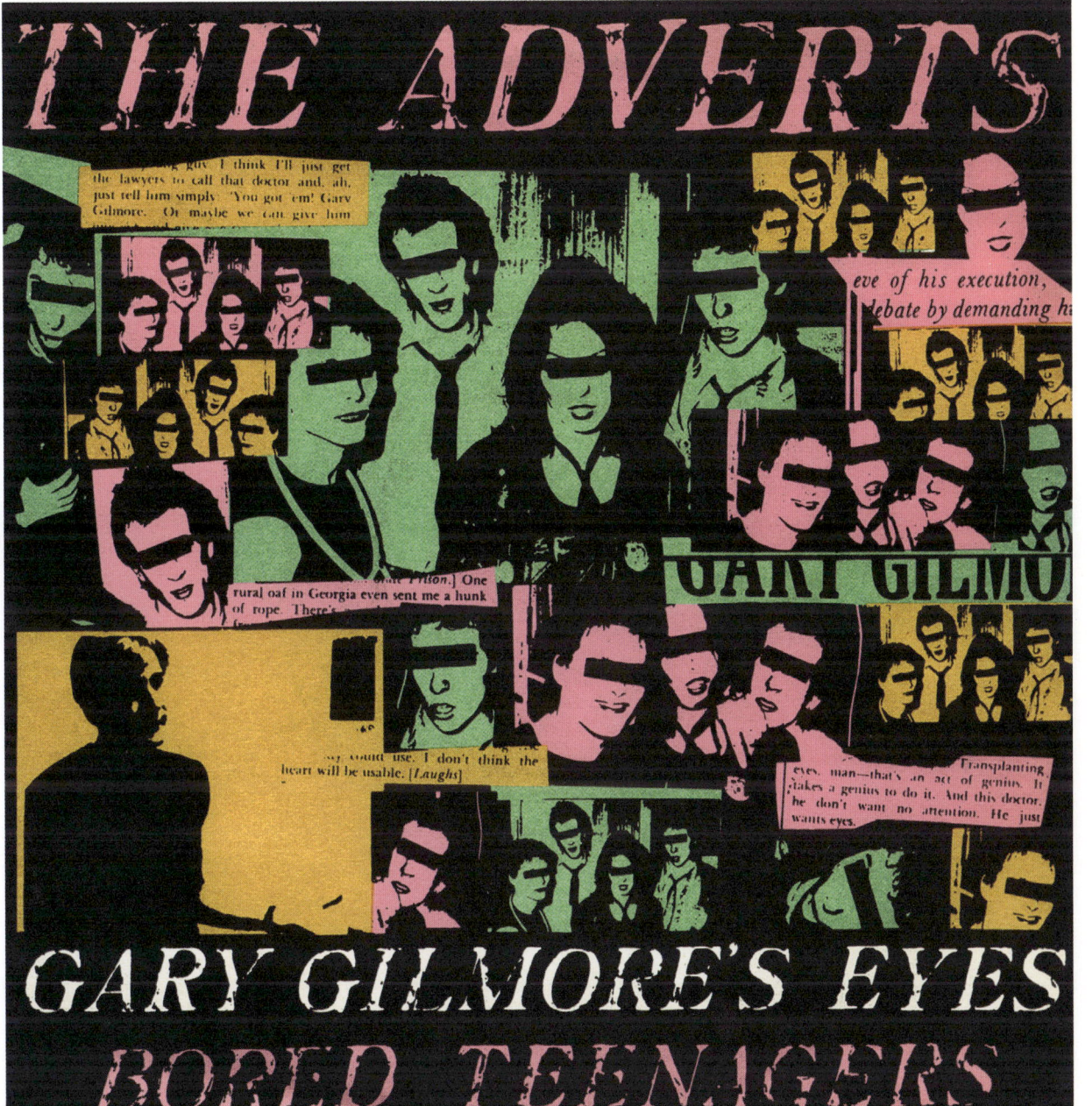

The Pogues
Fairytale Of New York

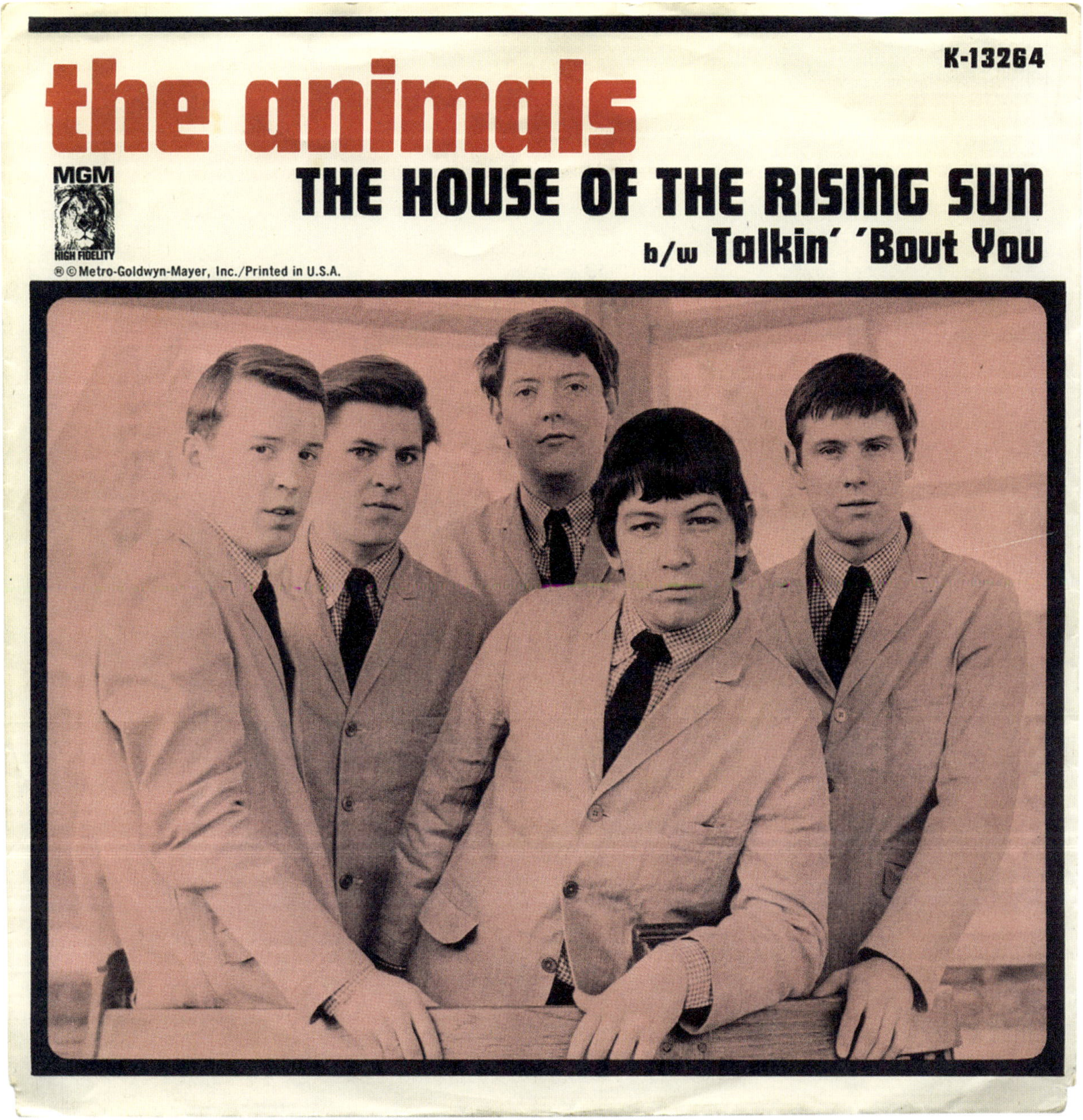

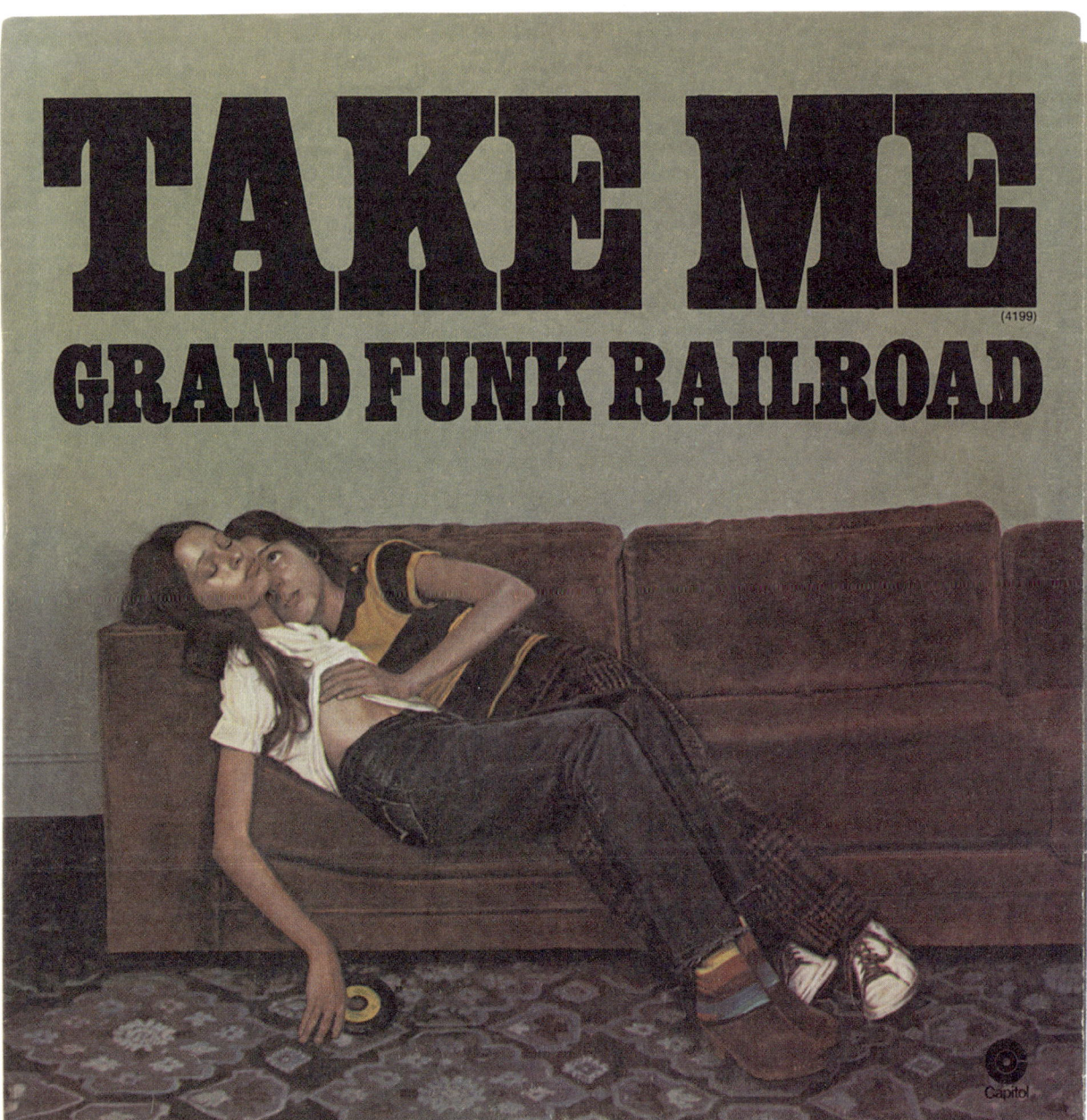

WILD THINGS BY THE CREATURES

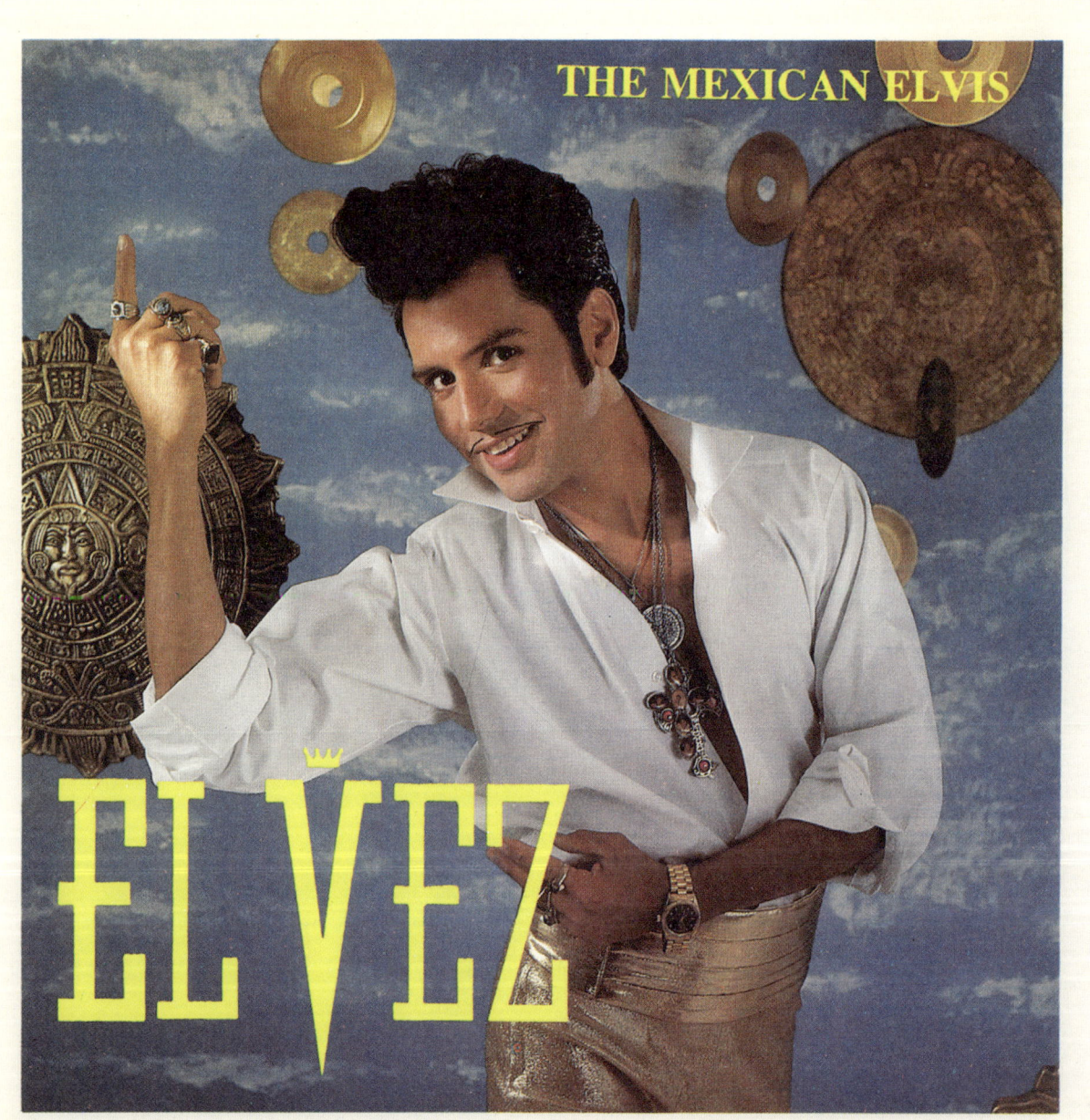

("TWIST" SPECIAL)
ROCK-A-HULA BABY
CAN'T HELP FALLING IN LOVE

45 RPM
RCA VICTOR
47-7968

Released by
POPULAR DEMAND
from
ELVIS' ALBUM
BLUE HAWAII
A PARAMOUNT PICTURE
A HAL WALLIS PRODUCTION

7968

© RCA Printed in U.S.A.

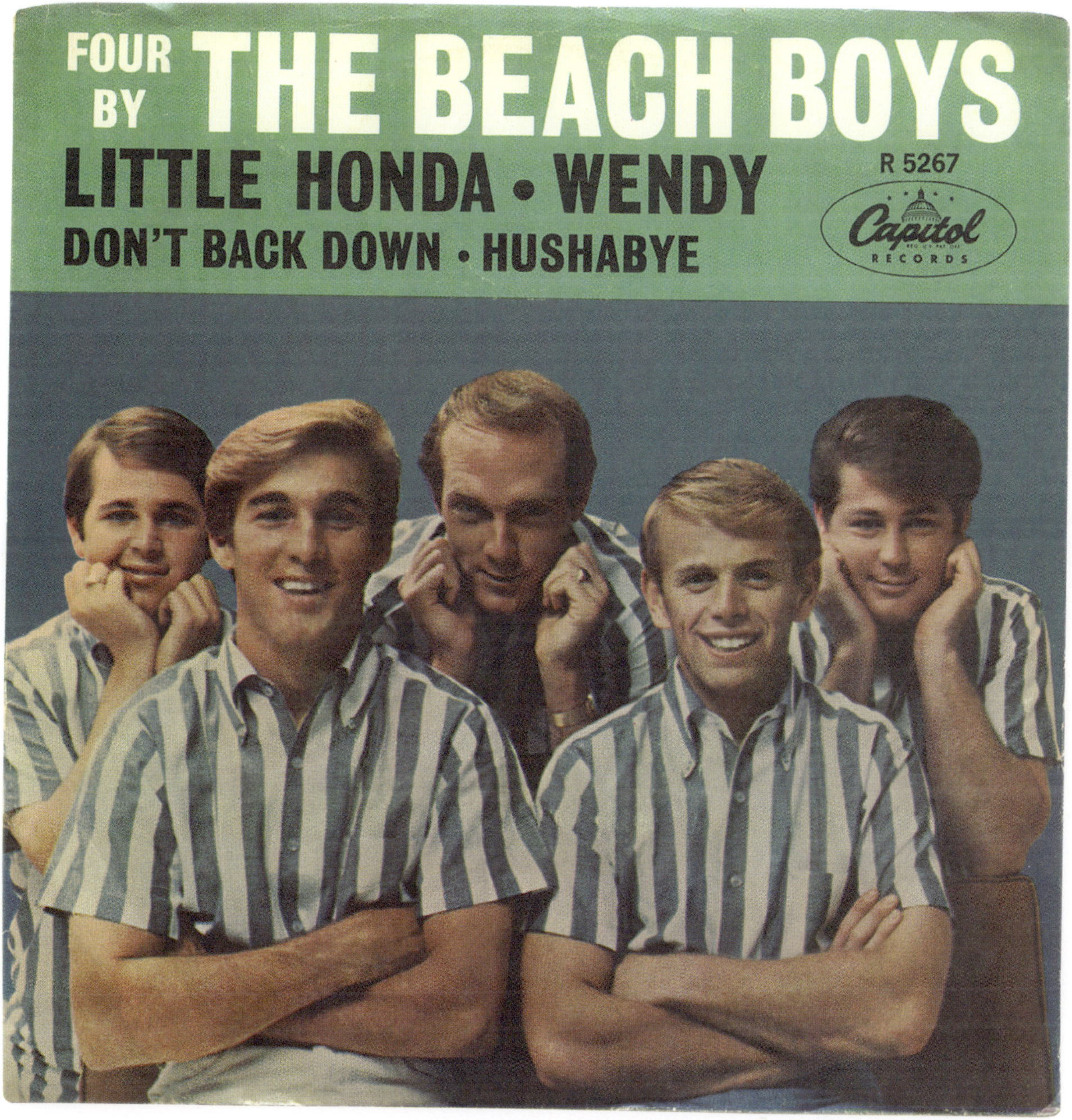

FOUR BY THE BEACH BOYS
LITTLE HONDA · WENDY
DON'T BACK DOWN · HUSHABYE

R 5267

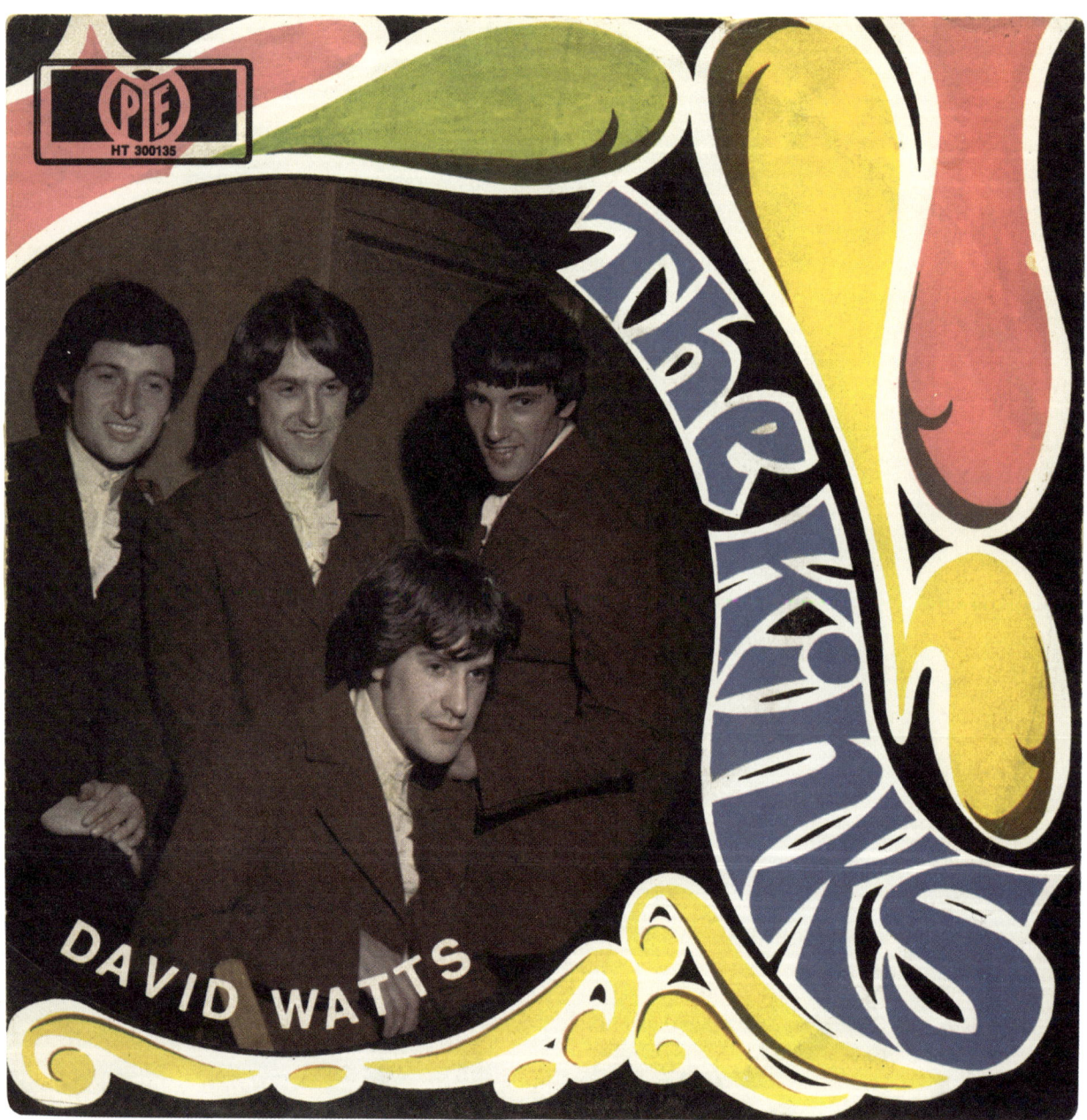

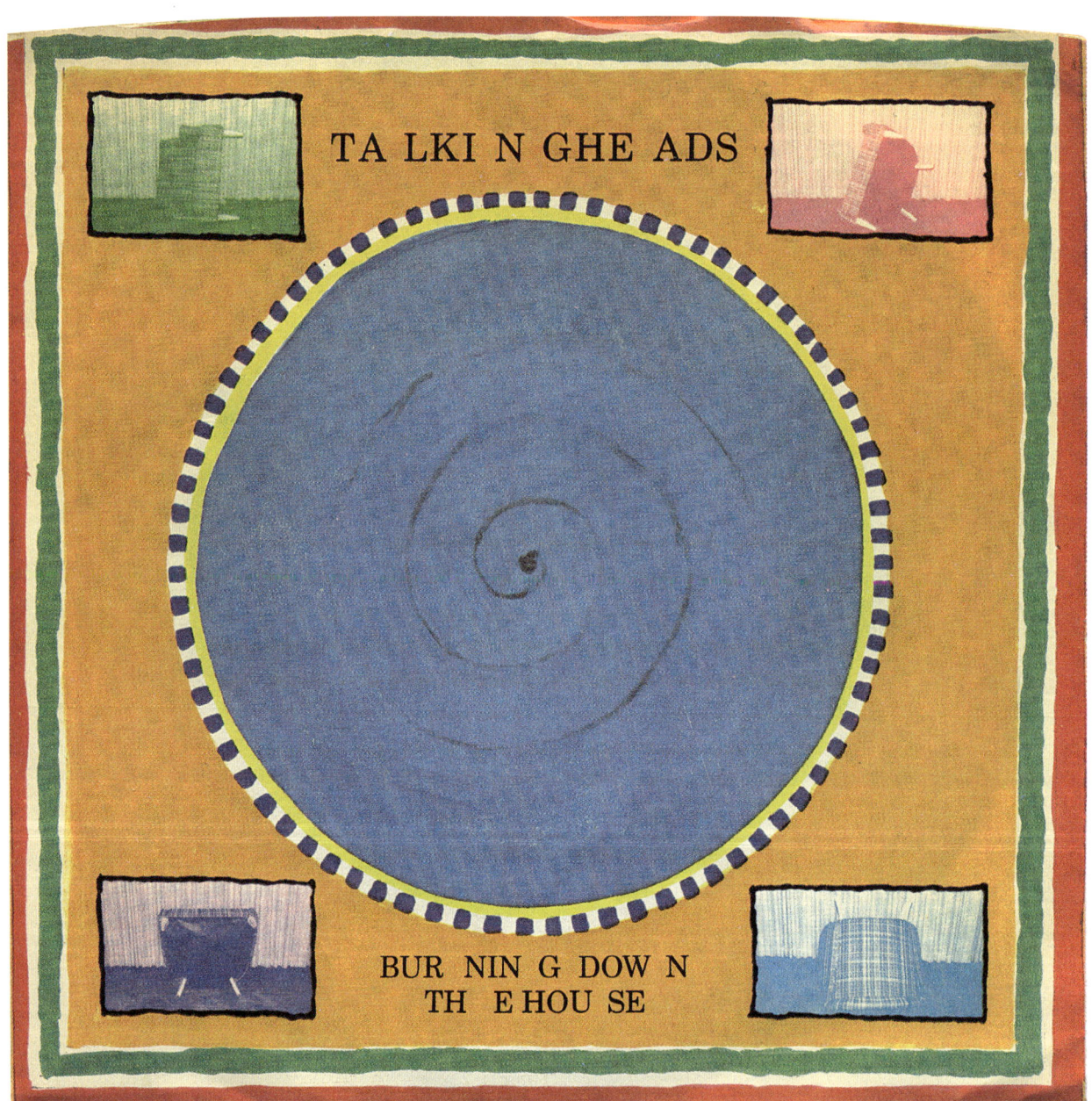

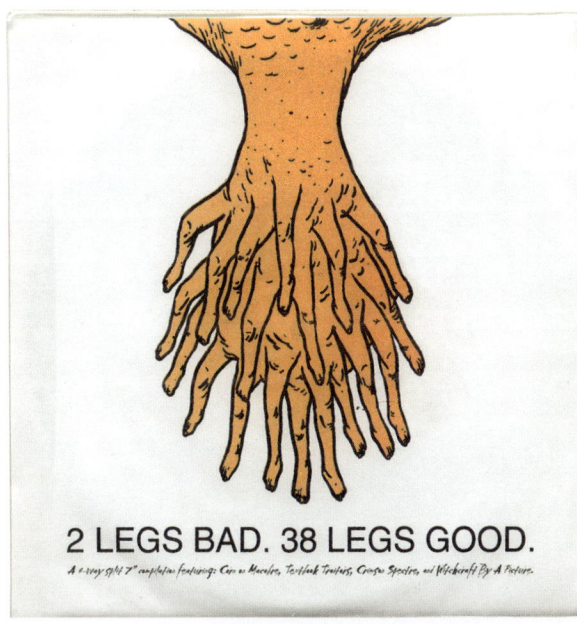

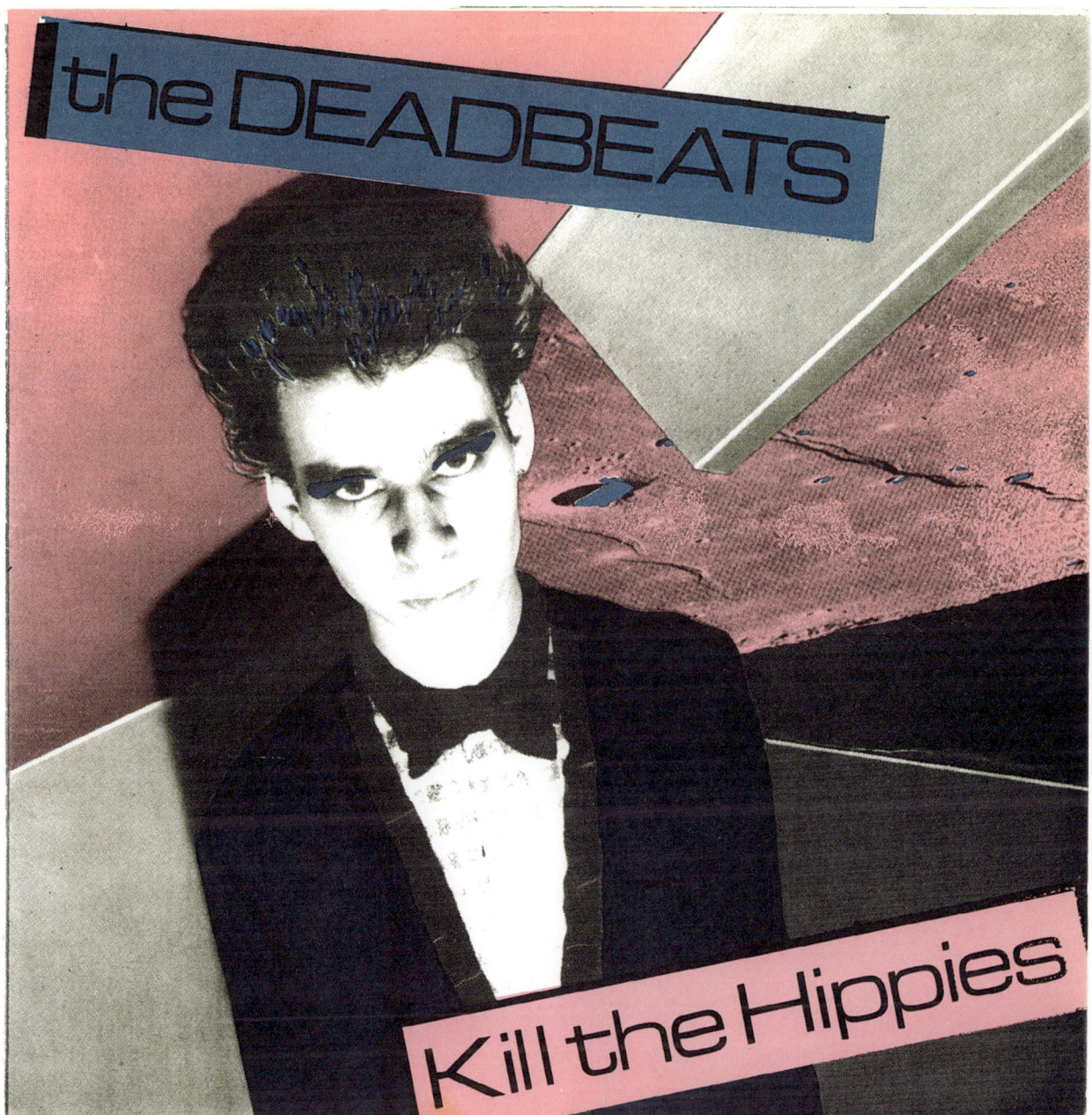

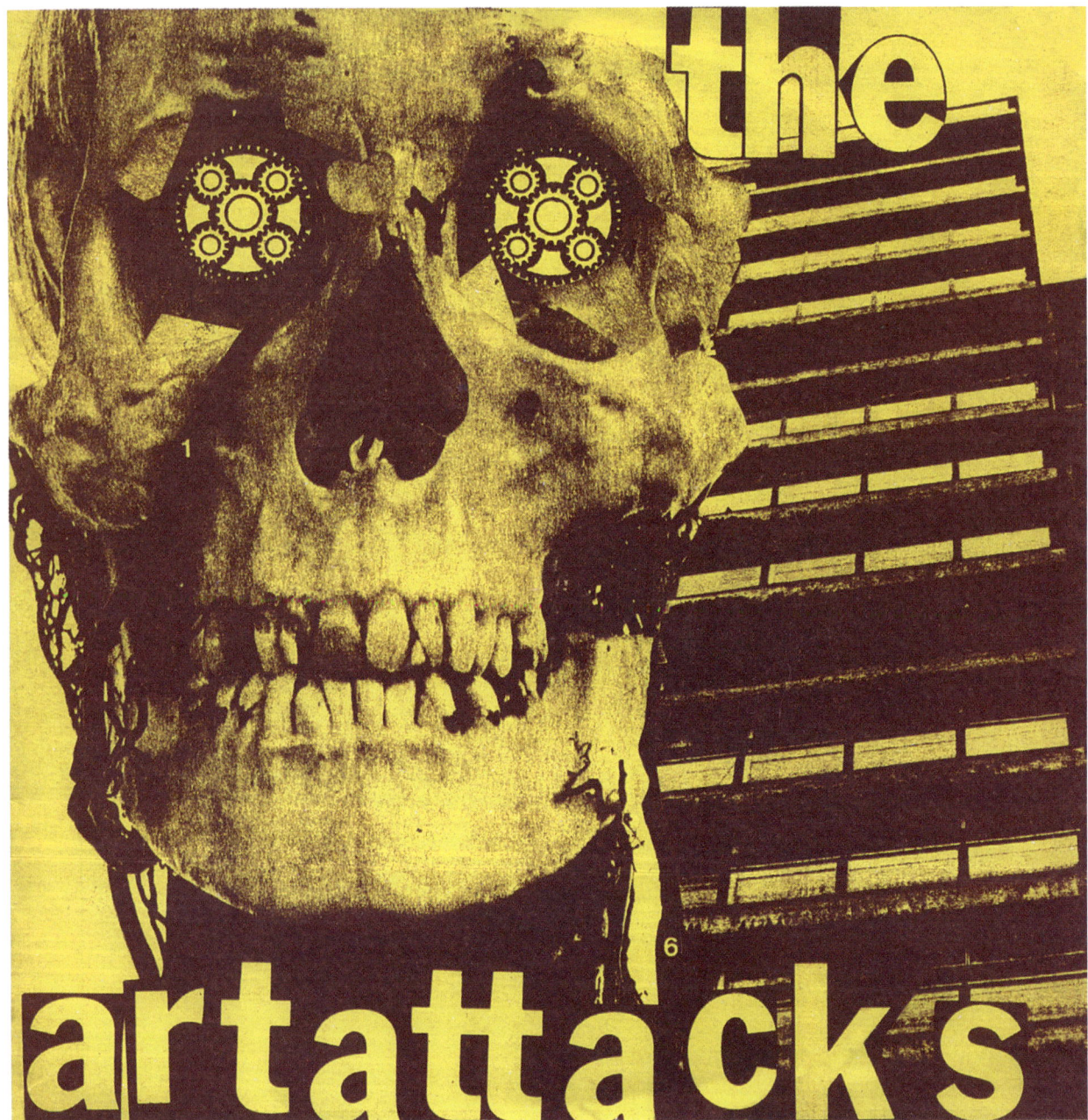

HAMMERHEAD
DUH, THE BIG CITY

GEORGE BURNS

I WISH I WAS EIGHTEEN AGAIN
3:22

ONE OF THE MYSTERIES OF LIFE
2:58

57011

mercury

℗© 1979 Phonogram, Inc. Manufactured and Marketed by Phonogram, Inc. A Polygram Company. One IBM Plaza, Chicago, IL 60611. Printed in U.S.A. Distributed by Polygram Distribution, Inc.

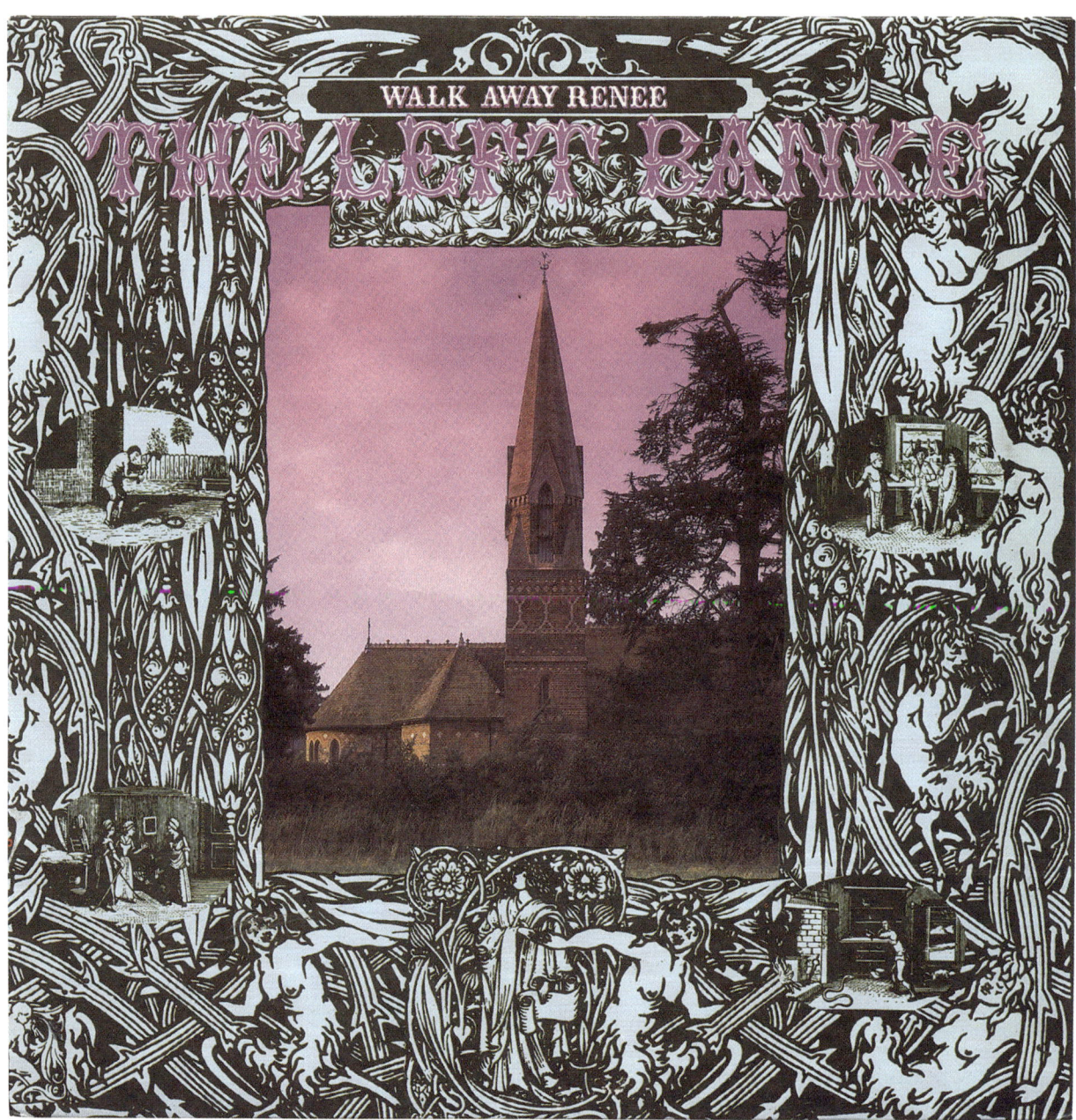

WONDERBREAD, HOT DOGS, FROSTED FLAKES, AND ELVIS

STUART GOLDMAN

The addiction began in July 1957 in a supermarket in Springfield, Massachusetts. I had just turned nine. Having been to this market many times with my father for groceries, I knew the layout of the store very well. Wonder Bread? Hot dogs? Frosted Flakes? I could lead the way. But on this trip, as we approached the dairy department, I spied something I'd never seen before. Within seconds, our shopping list became irrelevant. What derailed my young brain from thoughts of dinner (and into a dark realm of no return)? 45 rpm records, that's what. There, on a freestanding display by the milk and cheese, were records. Ricky Nelson, Chuck Berry, Sam Cooke, Little Richard, Buddy Holly, and Elvis!

I had certainly seen records in stores before, but up to this moment they had never seemed so accessible. I stood transfixed by the towering display rack, rotating it round and round. My developing power of logic suddenly kicked in: butter, eggs, bread . . . Elvis! I casually dropped the 89-cent picture sleeve of Elvis holding a teddy bear into the cart. After all, it was just another grocery item. When my father spotted it on top of the TV dinners, his response was quick and definitive: "No." He put Elvis back. I promptly returned the record to the cart. He put it back again. This game continued for a while, until my dad finally gave in and I had my very first 45 record and picture sleeve in one shot! Little did I realize what lay ahead.

Elvis Presley's "Teddy Bear" was one of more than ten thousand 45s I would acquire during the next fifteen years. Now, that is not a big number by collectors' standards, but nearly each disc or sleeve holds some kind of recollection. I am slightly embarrassed to admit I still have all these old records sitting alphabetized in metal cabinets today—each barely touched until Spencer and Judith came by to dig around for picture sleeves to put in this book.

My obsession with records and pop music dominated the latter part of my youth. In study hall, instead of Dickens or Brontë, I read *Billboard* or *Hit Parade* (my cousin Jane Heil was a staff writer and I got free copies). One day in 1960, while inspecting Woolworth's record department, I noticed some boxes on the floor. Curious, I bent down to discover piles of 45s inside with plain white labels marked "DJ Copy, Not for Sale." Here were brand-new releases sent by distributors to radio stations and some department stores in the hope that the songs would get played. Down on the floor, a strange sensation overtook me. Within seconds I crammed several dozen records into my duffle bag, getting a few future hits in the process. Fearing this would lead to a life of crime, I soon worked out a deal with a nice chain-smoking

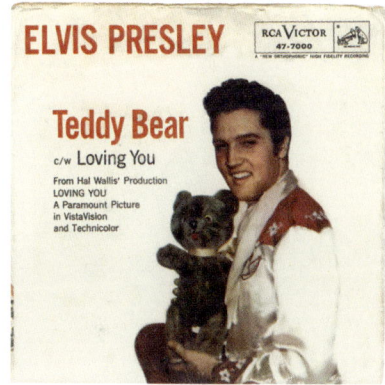

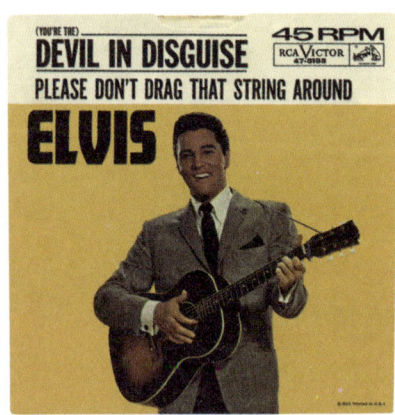

lady named Loretta at nearby Kresge's record department to actually buy new DJ records for just 20 cents each. The majority of these promo records, however, turned out to be bombs and never got played by anyone (except me). So ultimately I was forced to purchase the hits I couldn't get from the promo piles at the full discount price of 68 cents—luckily, those guys came with picture sleeves.

Unlike the plain paper DJ sleeves, 45 picture sleeves functioned as a kind of primitive music video. They made playing the record a more complete experience: you didn't just listen to a song, you actually imagined the artist singing it to you. Take Ann-Margret's RCA sleeve for "Gimme Love" from 1961. She certainly wasn't my favorite female singer; in fact, she probably should have stuck with acting. But who cared? She was gorgeous on that sleeve—even in black and white! Her picture definitely made the record sound a whole lot better. A few years later, the Ronettes, with the help of producer Phil Spector, improved on the concept with hot picture sleeves and records you actually wanted to play over and over.

The list of fresh young faces on picture sleeves goes on. Bobby Rydell definitely had some of the most striking picture sleeves of the era, mainly because the color was so saturated.

Cameo-Parkway Records must have really poured the ink on. And who could forget the Beach Boys' sleeves? Arranged chronologically, they can be used as an evolving style guide for young men's fashion, hair, and cars. Looking great was key on those early picture sleeves—being sexy and well dressed translated into record sales. That was certainly the case for Fabian, that fifteen-year-old kid they found sitting in front of his house in Philadelphia looking pretty. He couldn't really sing, but with solid pop songs and a picture sleeve that showed off his killer good looks and extensive velour shirt collection, he produced three Top 10 records ("Hound Dog Man," "Tiger," and "Turn Me Loose") like that.

Speaking of heartthrobs, everyone was thrilled when the Beatles came along in 1964 and changed everything—including sleeve art. Don't get me wrong, I love the Beatles as much as the next guy, but their entrance on the scene marked the end of an era of 45 sleeves as far as I can tell. Sure, being cute still mattered, but many brand-new marketing devices invaded record sleeves: shoulder-length hair, circus clothes, boots (made for walking), never-before-seen psychedelic colors, exotic body language, disturbed facial expressions and hair, not to mention the titles! (Would Pat Boone ever sing a song like "Psychotic Reaction"? Although thirty years later he did—look it up!) With the Beatles came a new type of sleeve—a new chapter in my collection.

I still look at my picture sleeves from the early days from time to time, and even play the records when I am really feeling nostalgic. So where did all this collecting get me? Well, I am the life of the party when it comes to rock-and-roll trivia. Flip side of "The Cha Cha Cha?" Hey, no problem. It is on Bobby Rydell's picture sleeve—"The Best Man Cried."

More importantly, collecting those sleeves gave me Elvis. With his voice, looks, talent, and unbelievable hits, he was my first role model; naturally I have every one of his early releases, which all came with picture sleeves (although they probably weren't really necessary to sell his records). I ended up producing documentaries, including one covering the story of Elvis' movies of the '50s (and the song "Teddy Bear" from his second film).

It is incredible how seemingly small things—an 89-cent grocery item casually dropped into your cart—can have such a large impact on your life. I'll be forever grateful that my dad let me keep Elvis and the Bear, and didn't make me put it back on the rack next to the milk and cheese.

45 PICTURE SLEEVES FUNCTIONED AS A KIND OF PRIMITIVE MUSIC VIDEO. THEY MADE PLAYING THE RECORD A MORE COMPLETE EXPERIENCE.

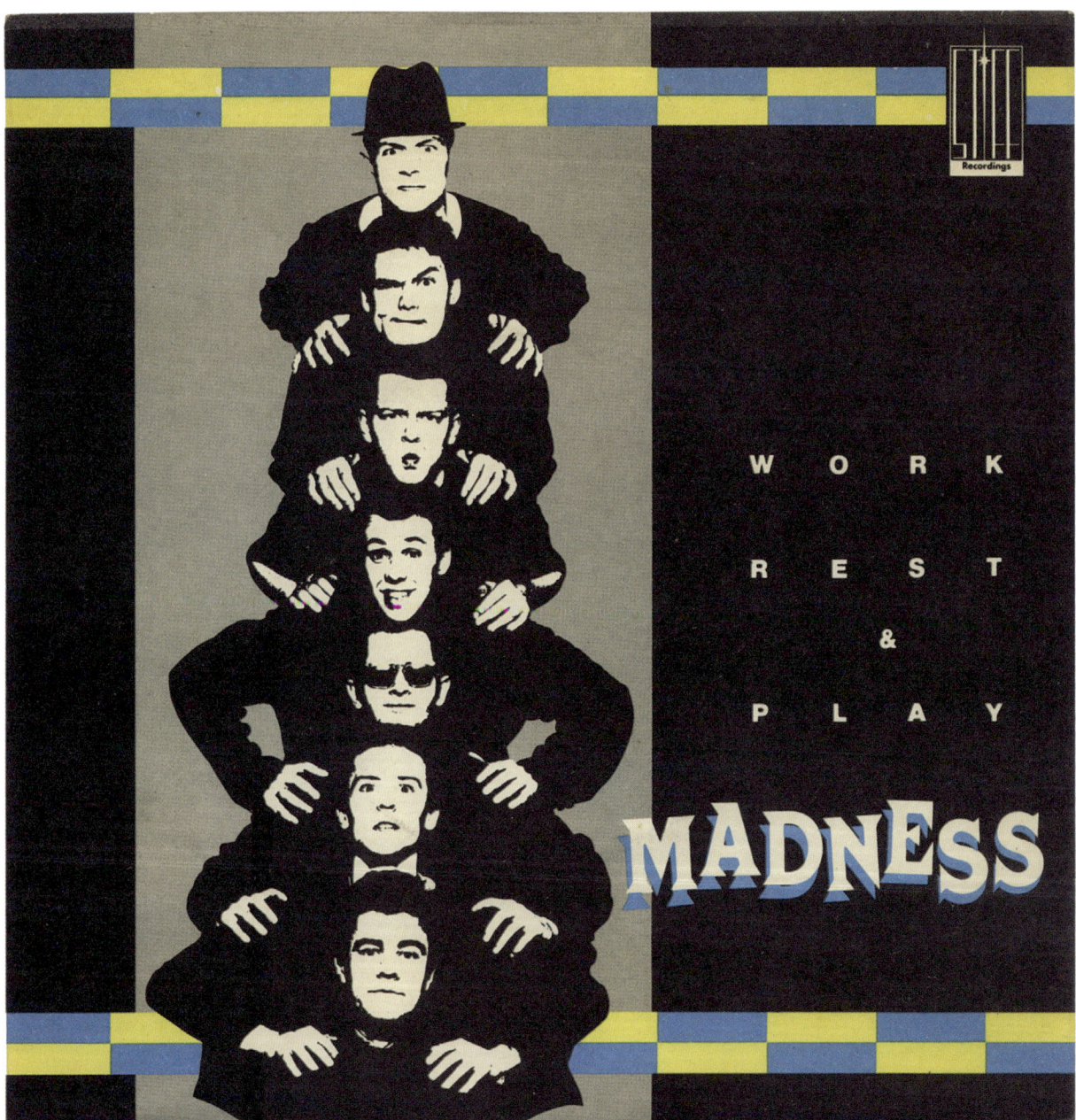

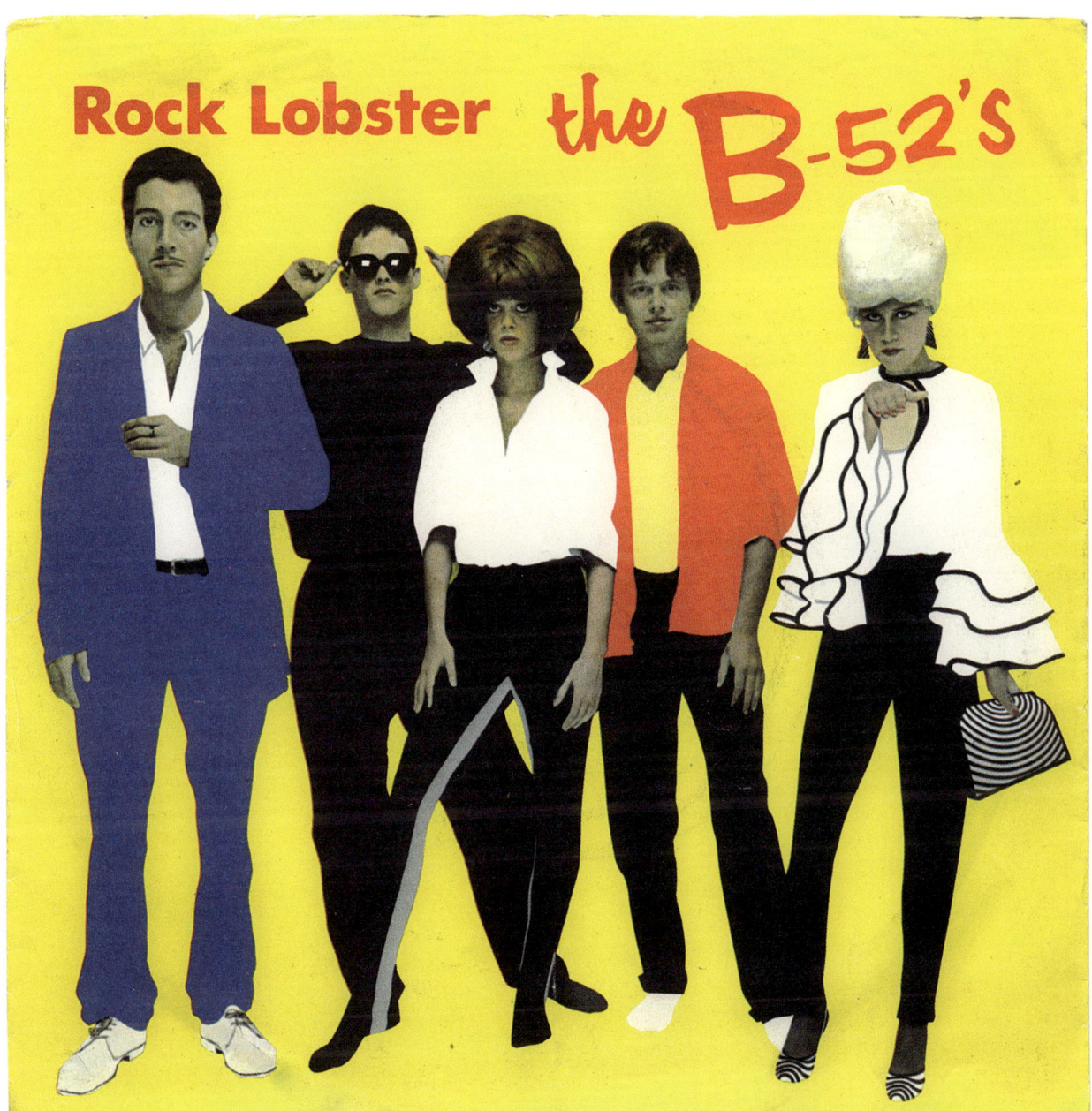

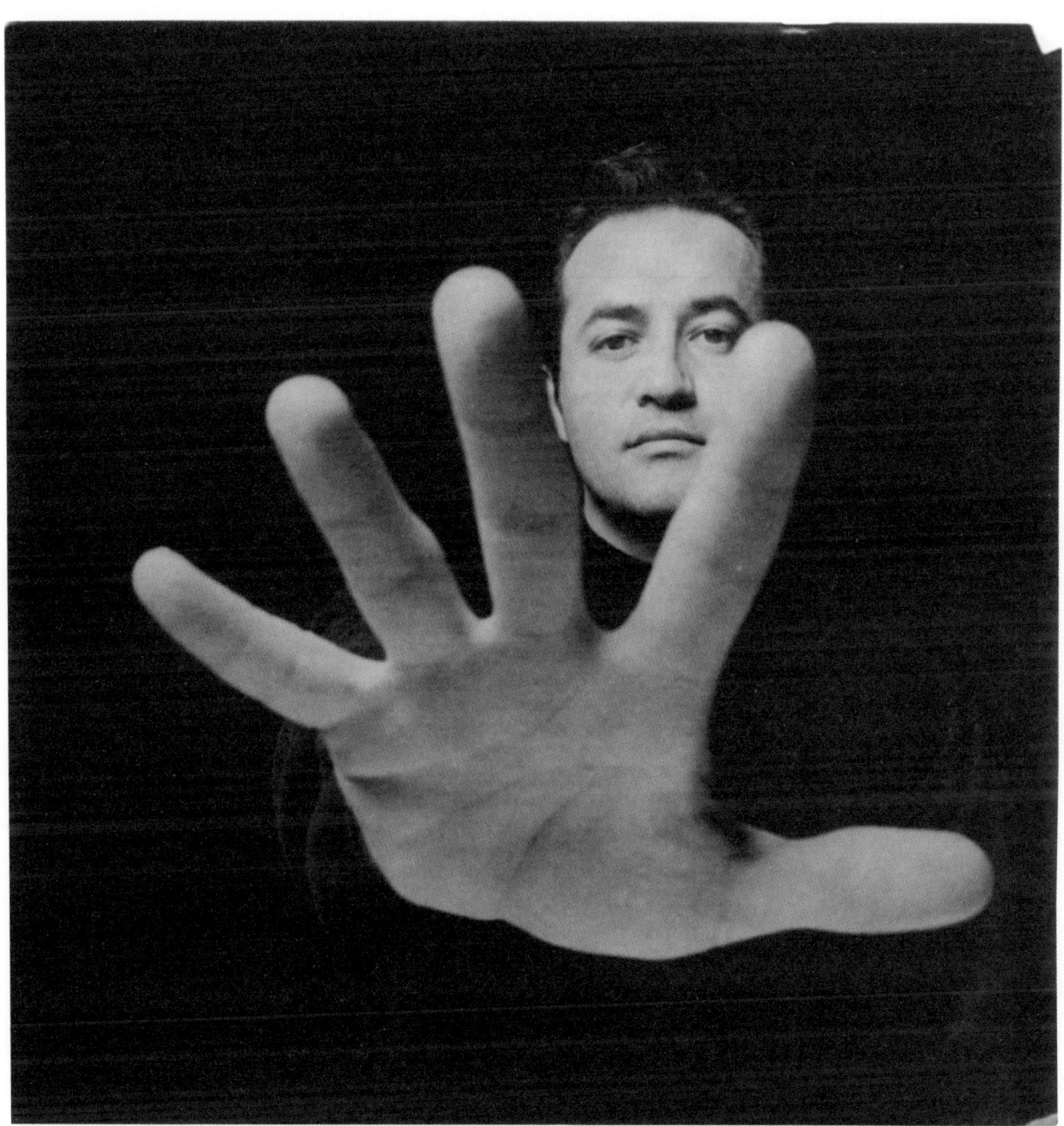

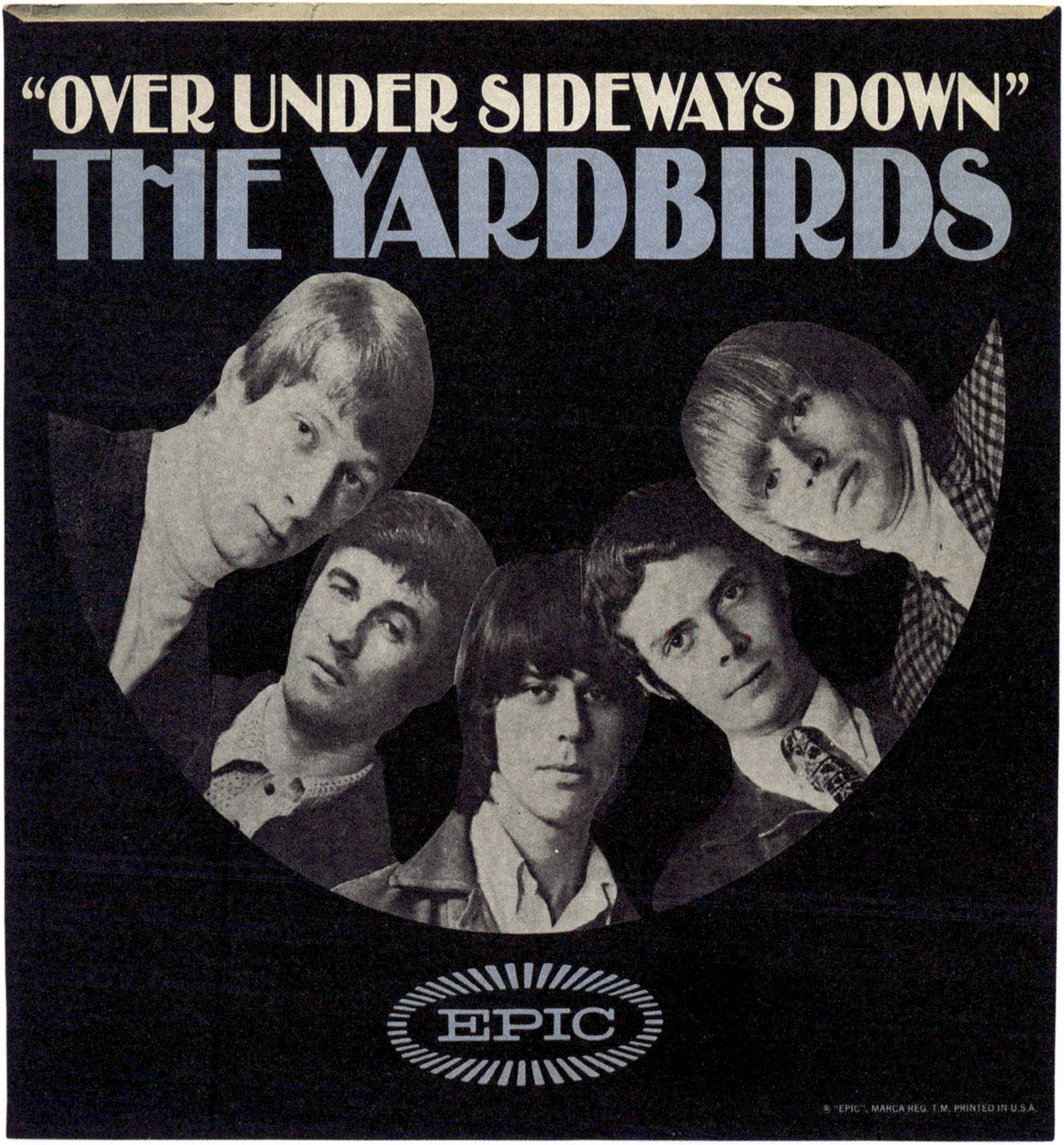

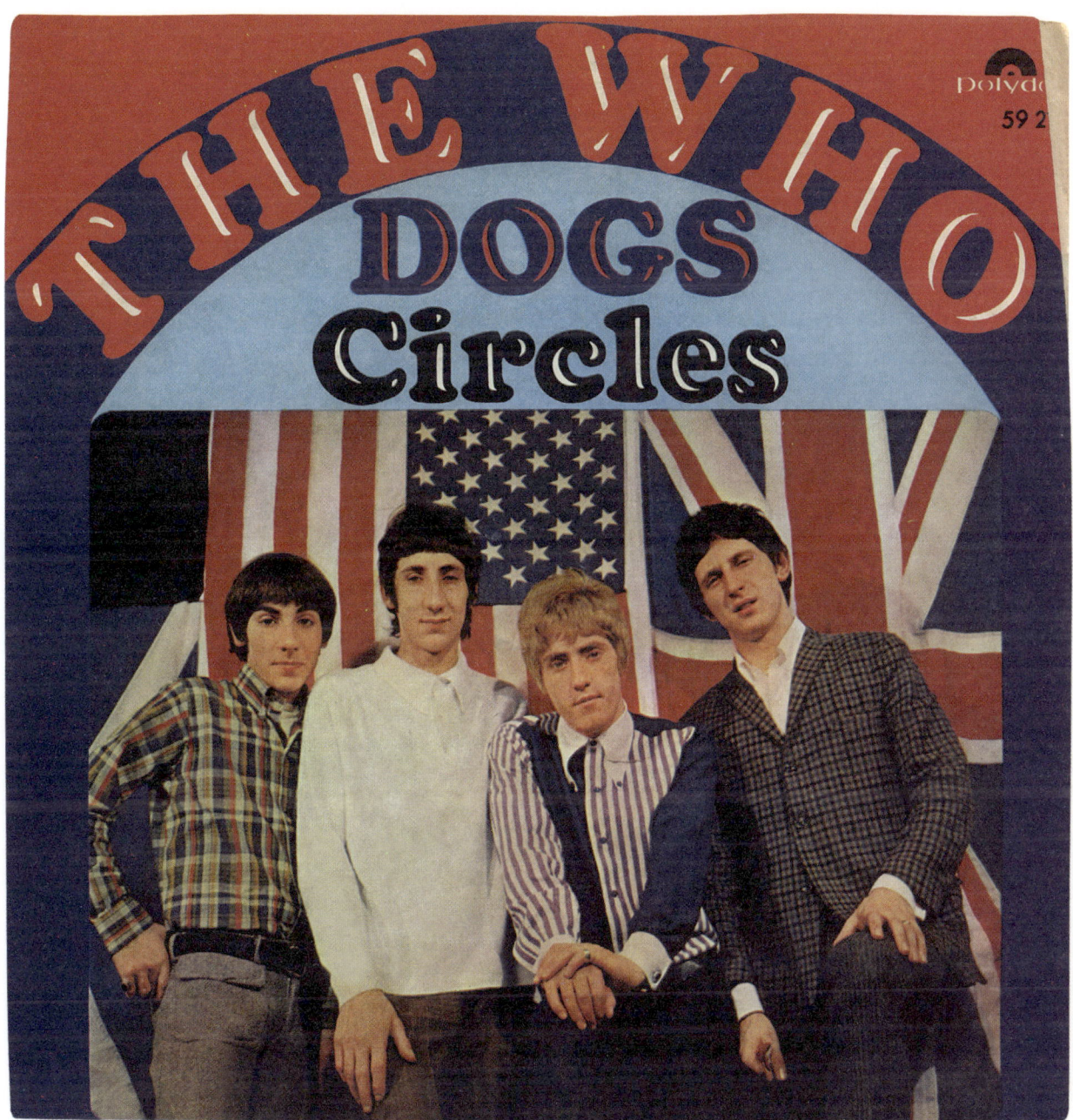

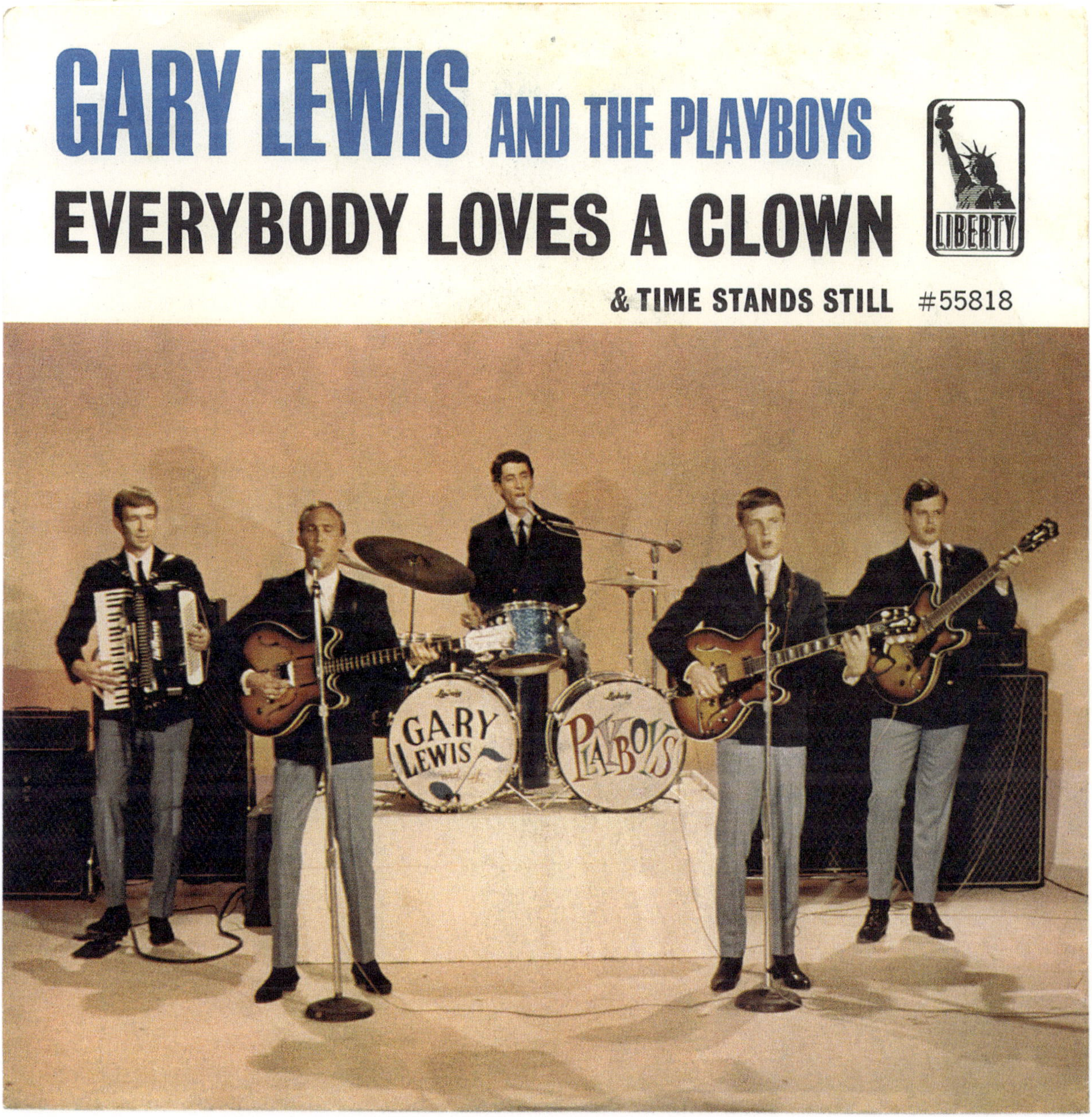

GARY LEWIS AND THE PLAYBOYS
EVERYBODY LOVES A CLOWN
& TIME STANDS STILL   #55818

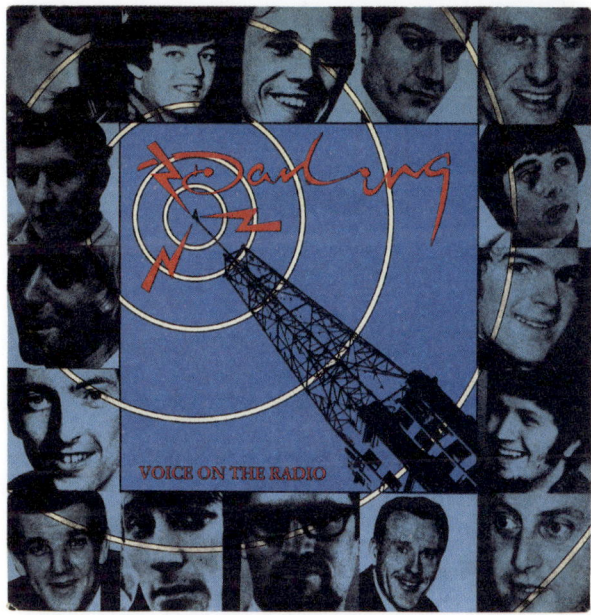

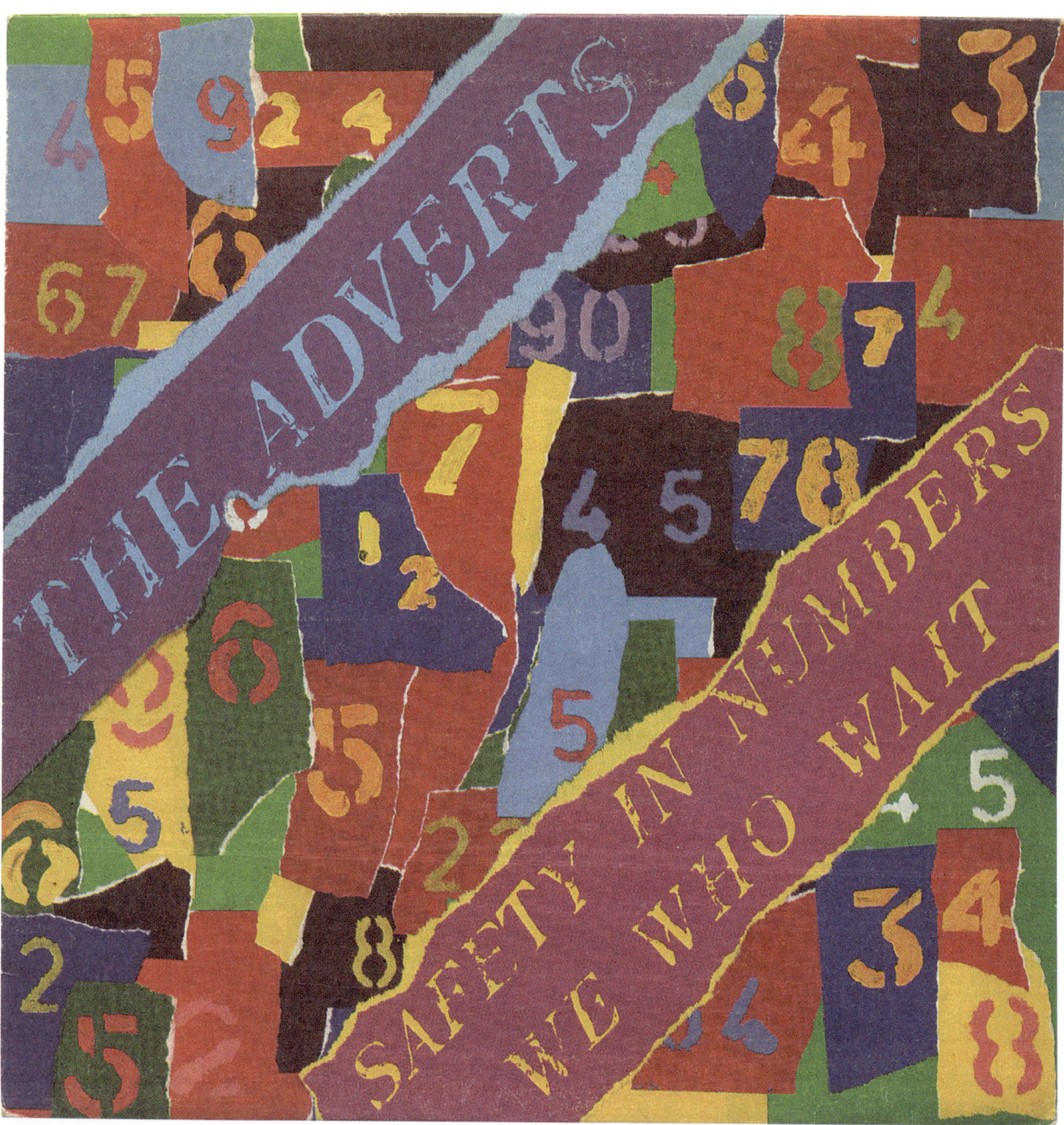

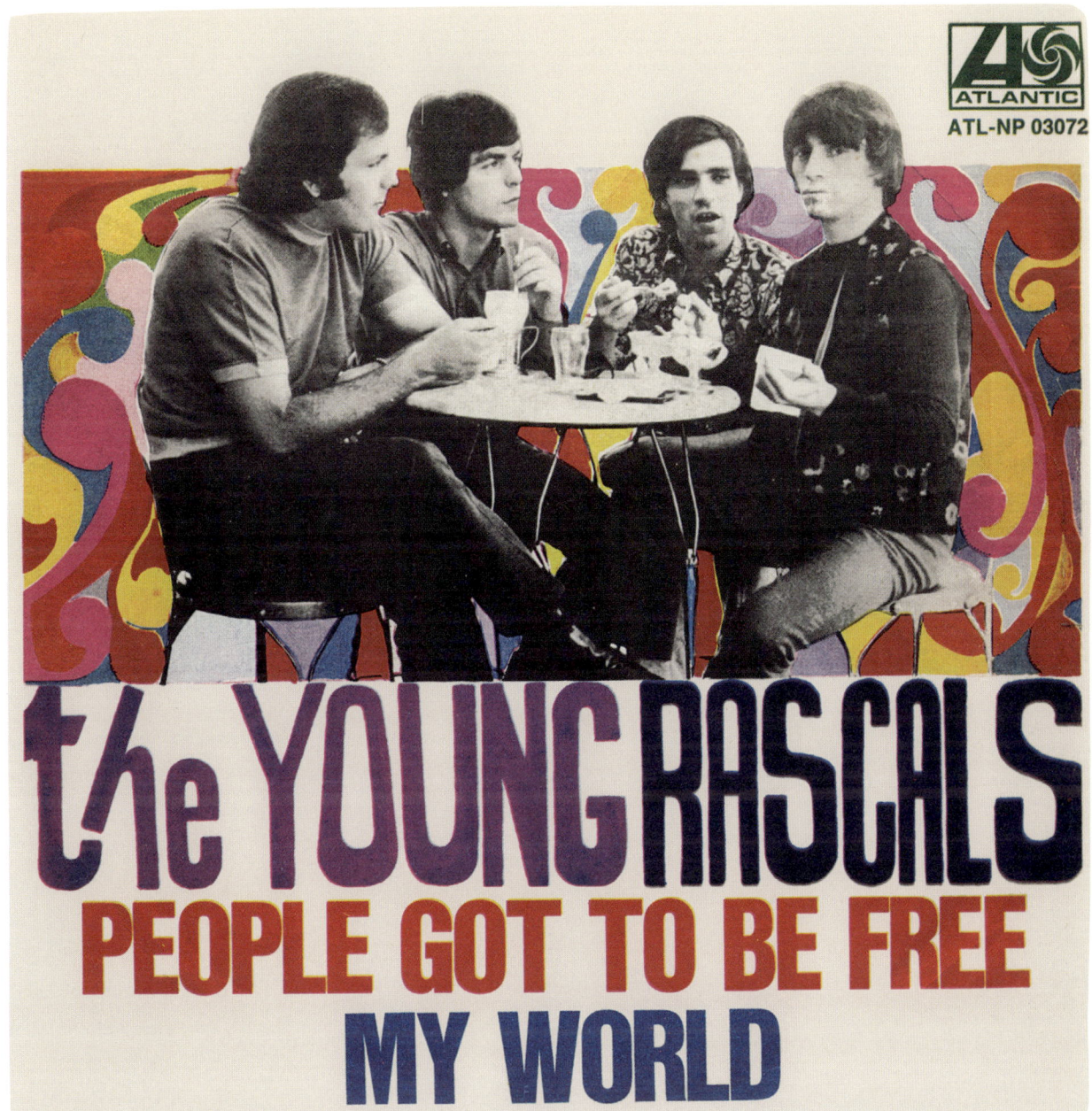

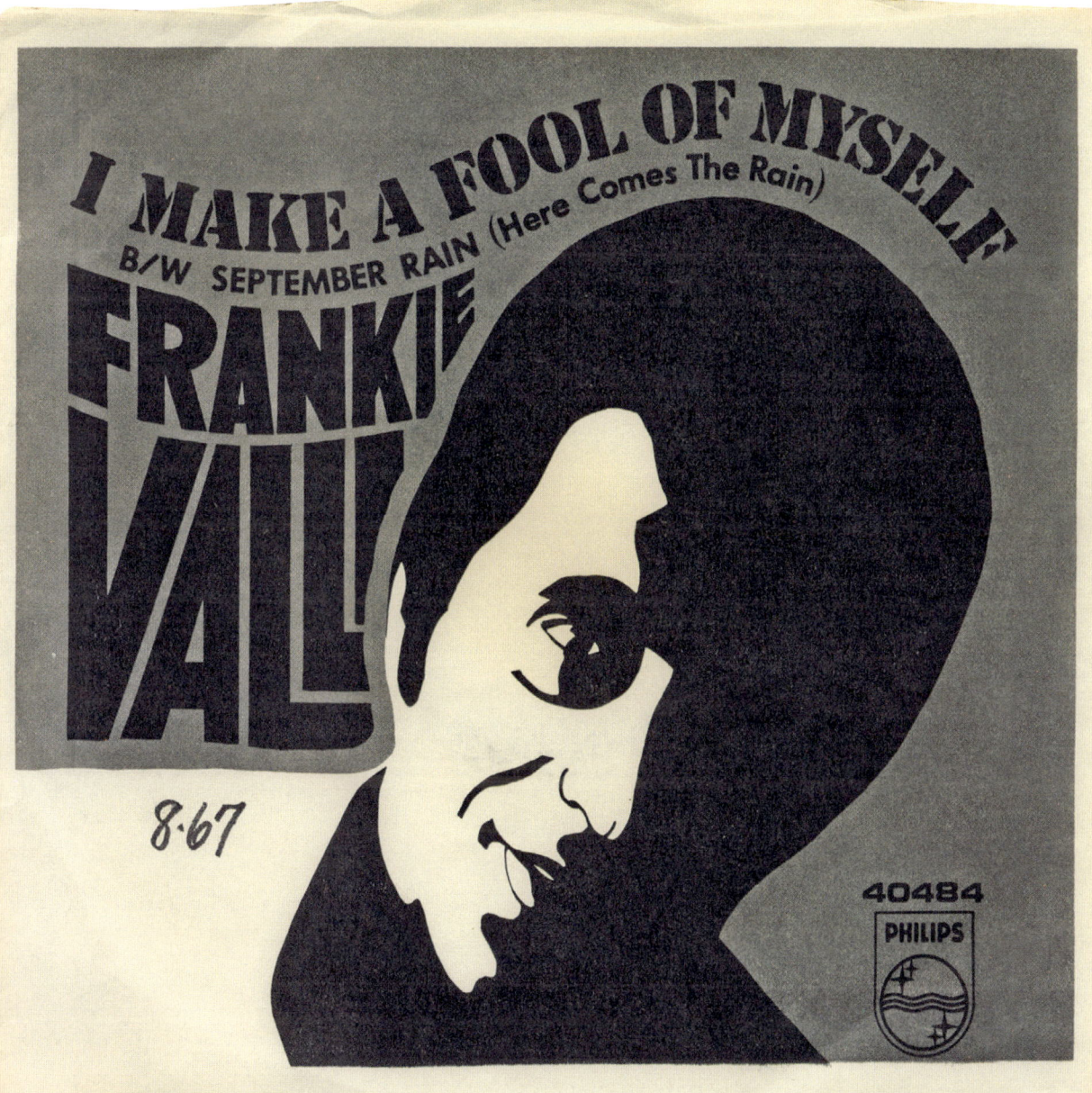

YOU KEEP ME HANGIN' ON
REMOVE THIS DOUBT

THE SUPREMES

MOTOWN 1101

FROM THEIR ALBUM—THE SUPREMES SING HOLLAND, DOZIER AND HOLLAND—MOTOWN 650

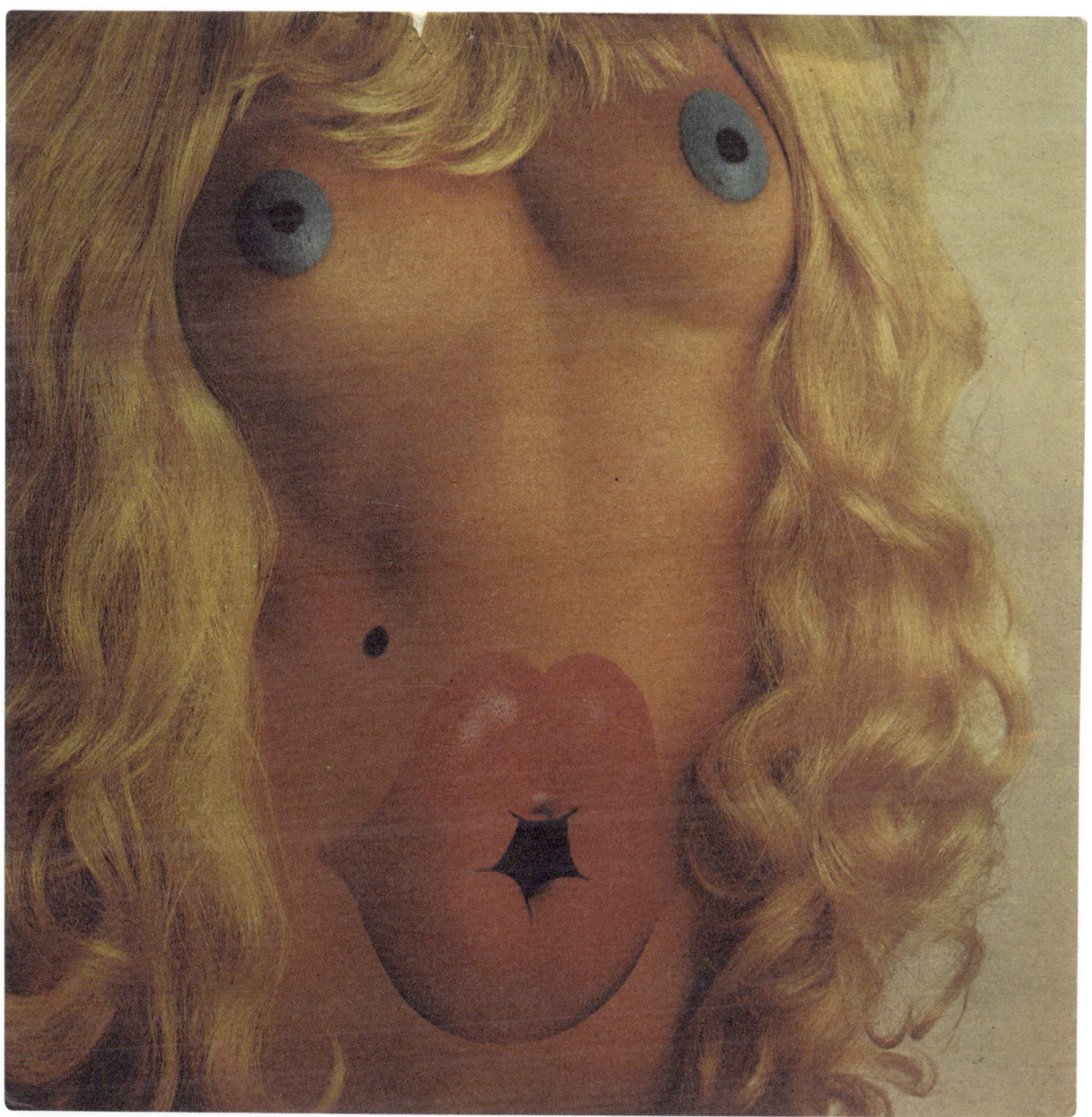

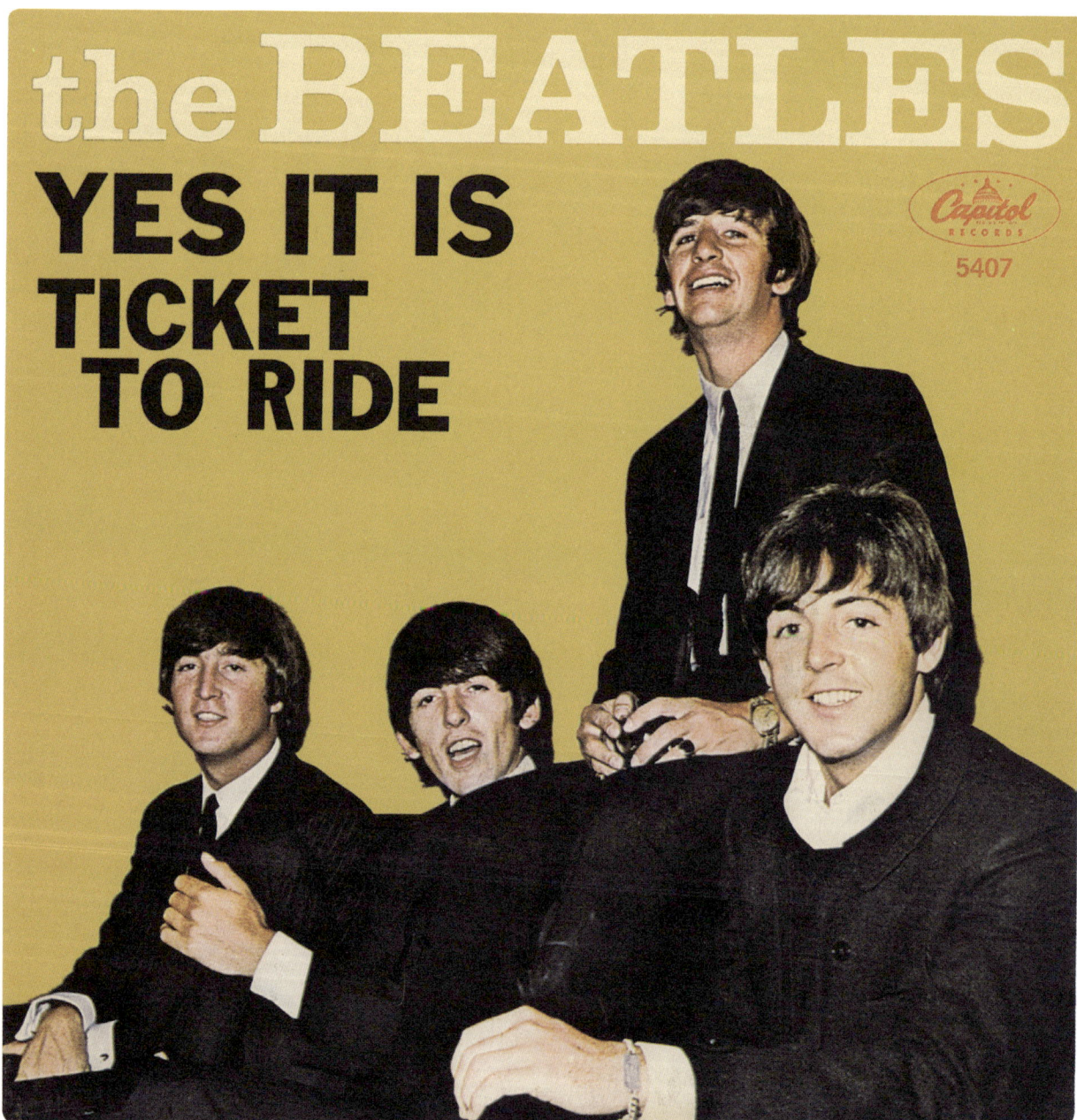

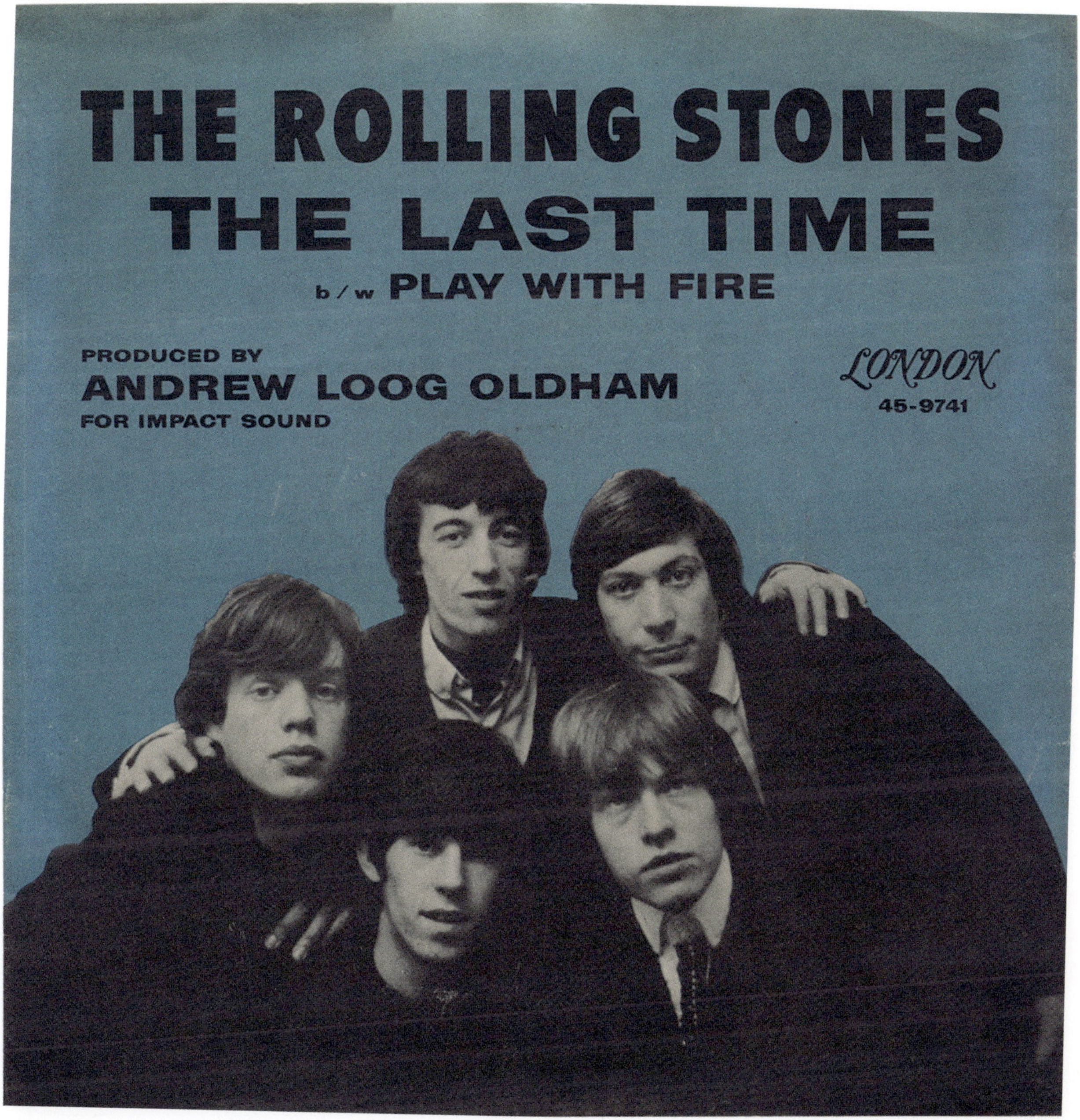

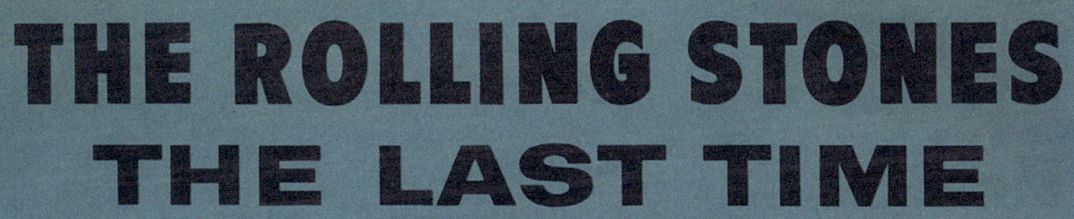

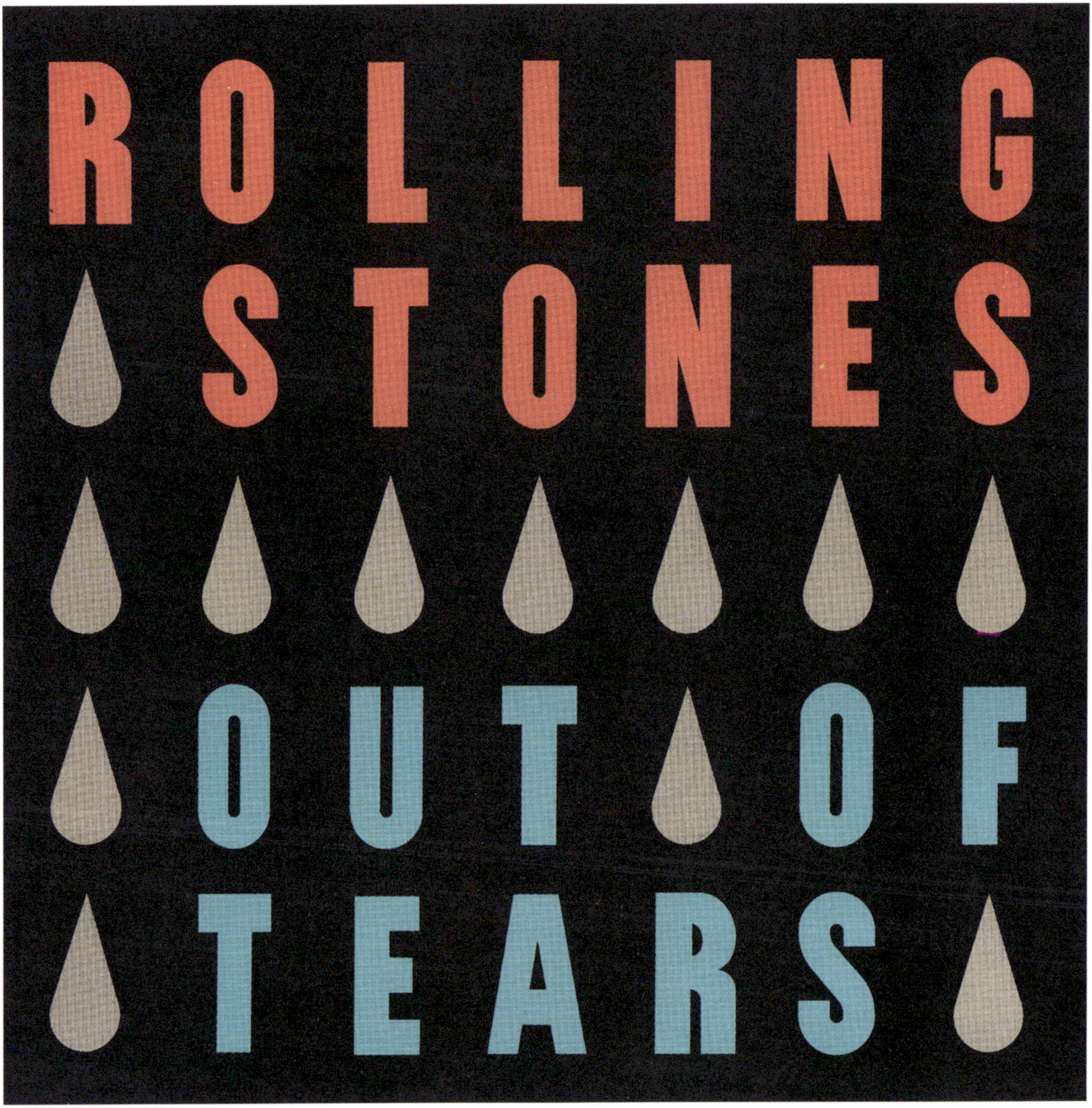

ROLLING STONES

OUT OF TEARS

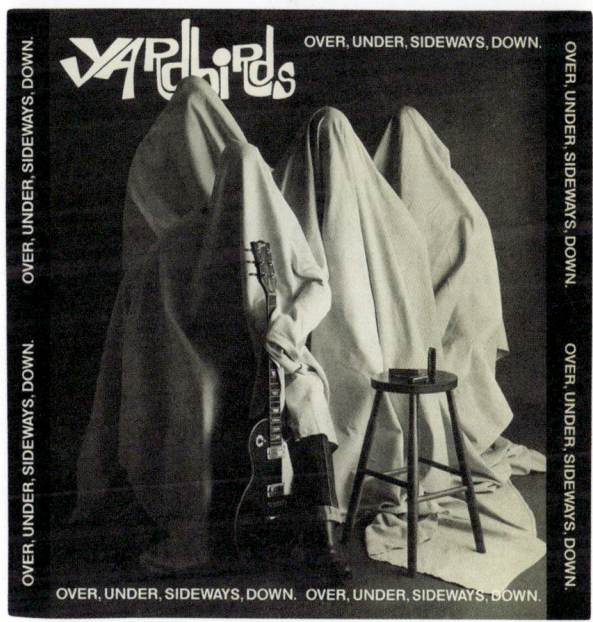

BULLMOOSE • DREAM LOVER
ATCO #6140

bobby darin

PHOTO: BRUNO OF HOLLYWOOD

WAZMO NARIZ

ACCIDENT
KILL THE BEE GEES

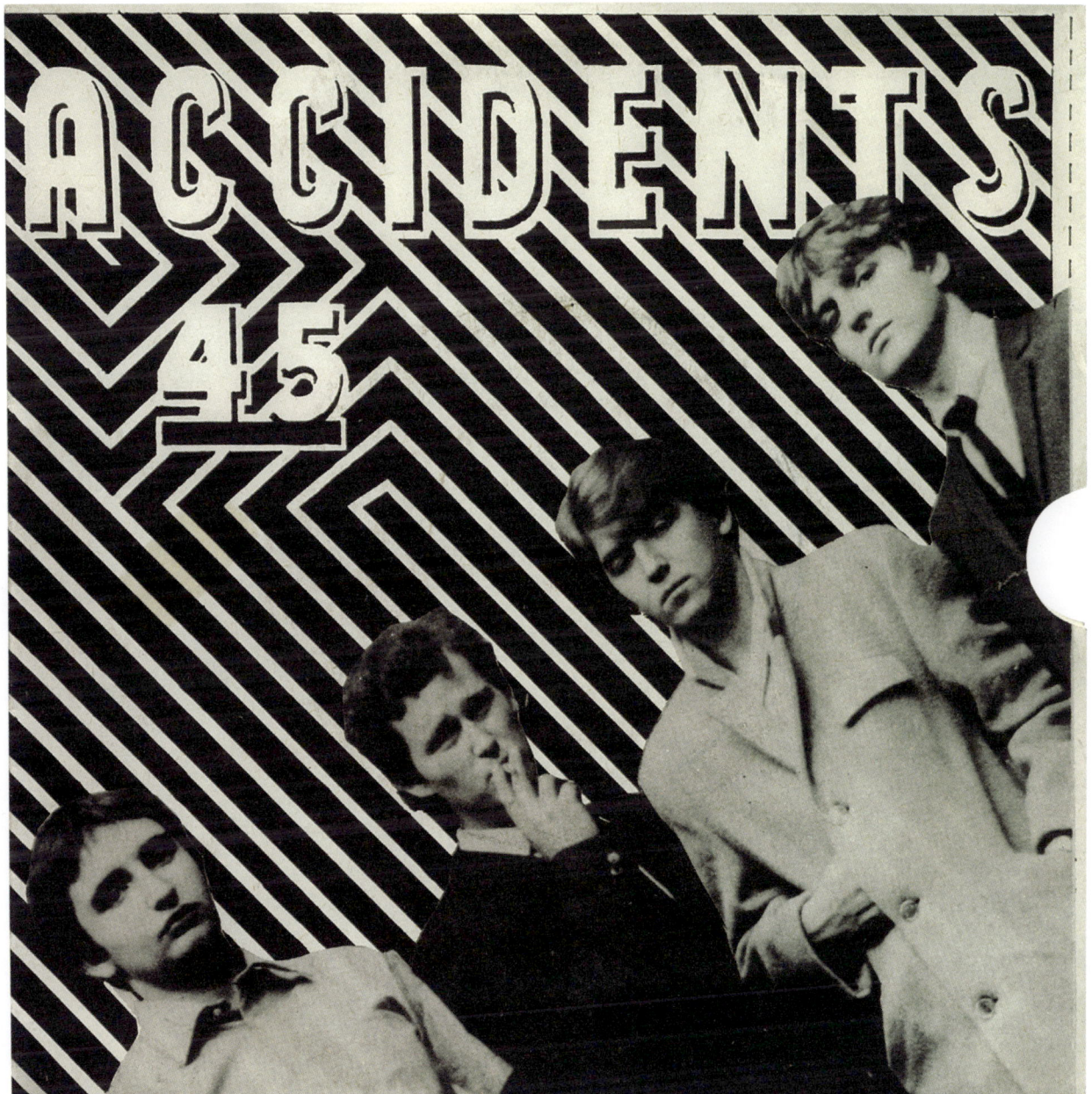

THE A-BONES

BUTTON NOSE
I'M SNOWED

DEAD KENNEDYS
Too Drunk To Fuck

singles GOING STEADY | THE WORK OF JEFF KLEINSMITH

JOHN FOSTER

A curious mix of shy and confident, playful and serious, in your face and enigmatic, the work of Jeff Kleinsmith is much like the man himself. Initially chiseled from the nervous rush of transformation that overtook the sleepy Northwest in the early '90s, his work has settled into an engaging body of evidence that a master walks among us—though he would surely blush and hide behind his thick shock of hair should you tell him so. Jeff's remarkable professional arc has shown an incredible ability to grow and refine, making it easy to forecast more innovative and extraordinary work from him in the future.

His destiny seemed to take hold at an early age. "I remember being really entranced by my mom's Janis Joplin and Woodstock Live records. CCR's *Cosmo's Factory* and John Denver's *Greatest Hits* also held particular interest for me," he says. "I'm not sure why, but I spent hours looking at my mom's records. As soon as I was able to walk to PayLess by myself I was buying 45s; "We Are The Champions," "Thunder Island," "Sometimes When We Touch," "Lady," "Dreamweaver".... I fucking loved those things. I played them over and over. It was definitely the music, but it was also the record collector side of me that loved the little sleeves and putting them in boxes and alphabetizing them." Later, an outside influence would wipe away his pop gloss. "When I was thirteen, my best friend's older brother couldn't take our AM radio crap anymore and one night he tried to scare us with Black Sabbath," Jeff recalls. "It actually changed me forever, for it was impossible to listen to those 45s the same way again. For an 8th grader, he had a crazy amount of LPs and posters and 45s and if I was meticulous, he was downright obsessive. It was really something else. Huge inspiration for me, as I immediately began to collect LPs. Seven years later I would start my 45 collecting again, when I got turned on to Sub Pop Records."

It was a circuitous path, but Jeff eventually found himself sitting in the Sub Pop offices—the home of the very label whose records had captivated him years before. Now he stands as one of their longest tenured employees; he's art director—the man behind the visuals at this trailblazing company.

His love of vinyl is forever intertwined with the label's dedication to it. "I'm really proud of Sub Pop for never letting vinyl die. Even when money was tight in the '90s, it was still important enough for us to keep releasing our bands on both formats. 45s were huge for the label. The Singles Club was genius." The Singles Club was an update on the old record of the month club; Sub Pop released two 45s every two months

 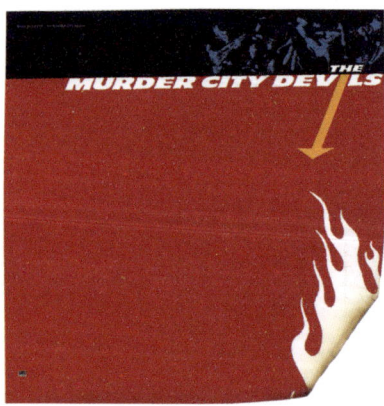

in late 1989 through the end of 1993 (and have reinstituted the club two more times since then). All releases were packaged for collectors—using special effects such as colored vinyl—and featured a veritable who's who of '90s alternative rock from all over the globe. The Singles Club was a wonderful moment in the history of the 45.

When pressed, Kleinsmith admits his favorite 45s of all time come from the same catalog. "You'll laugh, but it's probably Nirvana's 'Love Buzz' or Mudhoney's 'Touch Me I'm Sick,'" he admits. "Not particularly noteworthy in the design department, but the music had a huge impact on me. Very sentimental about those early Sub Pop singles. I love Art Chantry's Flaming Lips' 'Drug Machine' single. That one had a big impact on me design-wise."

Kleinsmith's love of album designers—such as Chantry, Reid Miles, Ed Thrasher, Hipgnosis, and Independent Projects—combined with his admiration for Push Pin Studios, Andy Warhol, Saul Bass, science fiction books, Polish and Cuban poster designers from the '50s and '60s, and pop culture in general resulted in a potent mix that would quickly crystallize and shatter away, leaving him to emerge with a style all his own.

As he moved forward in his career, 45 record sleeve design became a treasured avenue for experimentation. "Singles are really not that different than designing an LP. They are just slightly smaller squares. However, a big difference for me, as an art director here, is that bands tend to be a little less precious about the artwork, so we in the art department get to have some fun with the design and packaging. In a way, the 45 has a dual role as legitimate music release and as a cool promotional item."

One of the best examples of this is his work with the Murder City Devils. "It was early on that the idea of burning a corner happened," he explains. While this was an awesome idea design-wise, it would be a tricky production job. "I was working with the printer and he made a fantastic suggestion to trim most of the corner where the burning would occur. This meant that a lot less paper had to burn to get the effect we wanted. He provided a blowtorch and we went out to the alley and balanced 25 unstuffed single sleeves at one time under the lid of the dumpster and set to burnin'. Everything went well until they started selling like crazy and reorders were rolling in and we had to keep burning more!" he laughs. "It was a laborious process. Other staff members had to help out. You'd think burning shit would never be a drag."

That sense of experimentation runs through Kleinsmith's work. I force him to choose a favorite of his many innovative designs. "Oh, man, it's not very good, but it's probably the Jessamine single. It gets an A for effort. It was one of the first singles I did for Sub Pop after I was hired on officially. I came from the newspaper world, so packaging was exciting to me. Working with a little one-man printing operation called Thingmakers, we really pushed the envelope. This single has a little of everything: offset, screen printing, rubber stamping, one side of the many inserts is a puzzle of sorts, the outer sleeve folds up like a matchbook and the whole thing is held together with a bolt!" Later, Jeff tried this all again with more success on "the series of English singles we did (Elastica, Supergrass, Gene, Smash). Along the same lines as the Jessamine but more refined."

Kleinsmith's work is defined by that ability to experiment, learn, and adapt. No longer just a fresh face on the Seattle scene, but an acknowledged tastemaker around the globe, he never stops trying to ensure that his next project will be his best yet. And I'm sure it will.

HIS WORK HAS SETTLED INTO AN ENGAGING BODY OF EVIDENCE THAT A MASTER WALKS AMONG US— THOUGH HE WOULD SURELY BLUSH AND HIDE BEHIND HIS THICK SHOCK OF HAIR SHOULD YOU TELL HIM SO.

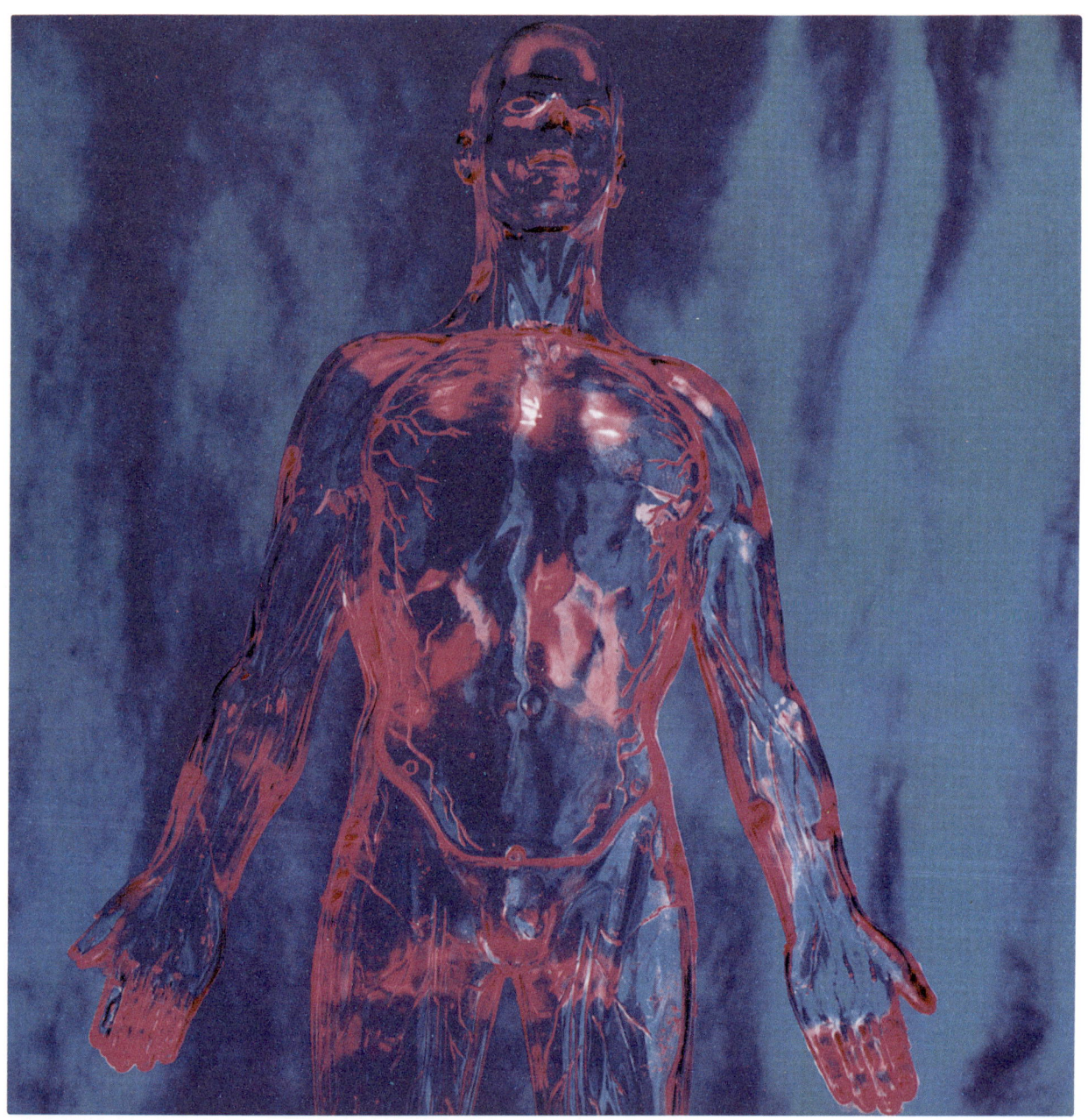

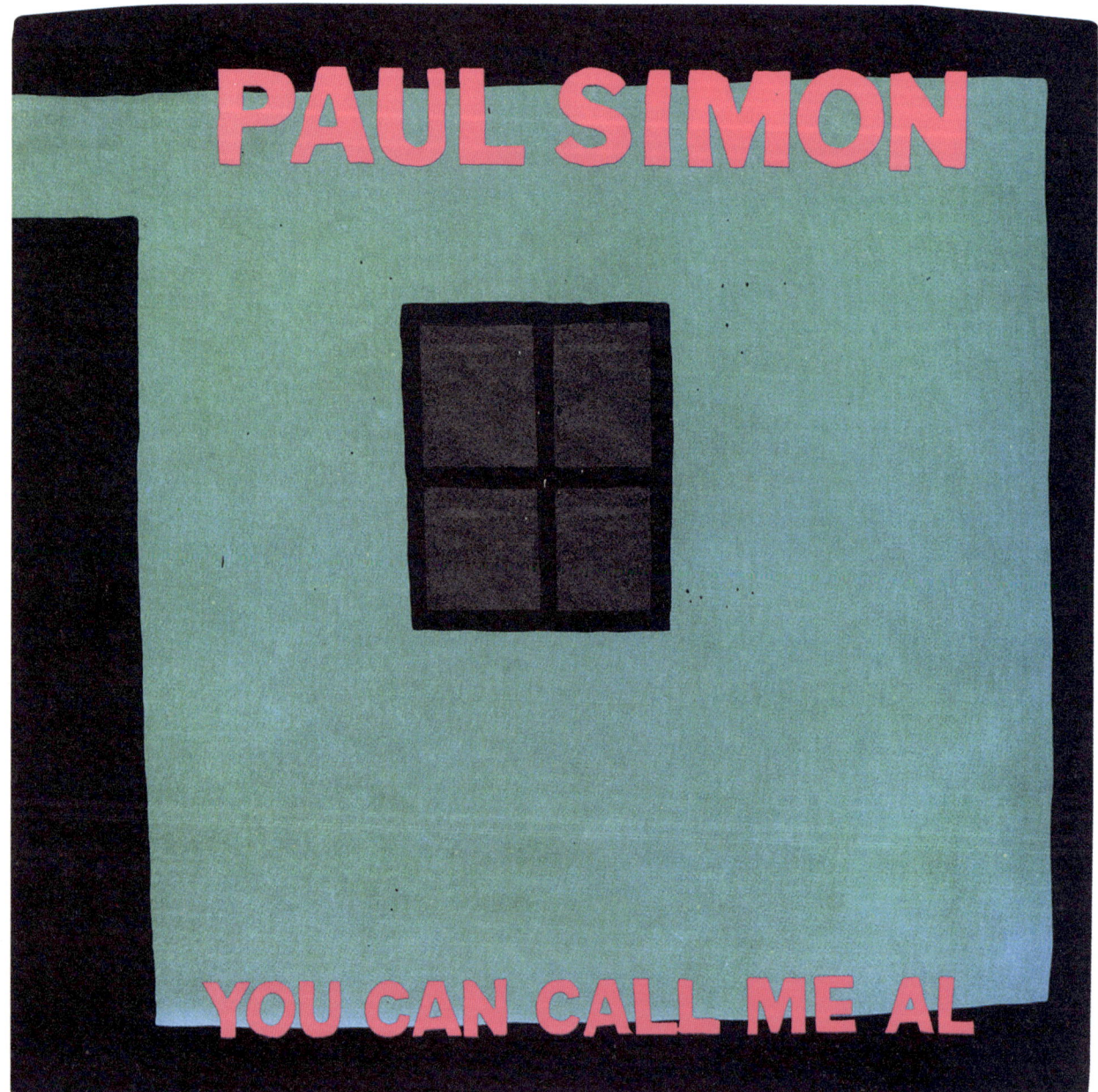

A "New Orthophonic" High Fidelity Recording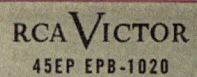
45EP EPB-1020

The Great Music Themes of Television

Hugo Winterhalter and his Orchestra

If I Could Tell You • In My Garden *(Voice of Firestone)*
Mama *(Mama)*
Smoke Dreams *(Chesterfield Supper Club)*
The Coca-Cola Company Theme

Music of Manhattan • Memories of Yesterday *(Kraft Theatre)*
Prelude to the Stars *(Studio 1)*
Melancholy Serenade *(Jackie Gleason Show)*
Seems Like Old Times *(Arthur Godfrey)*

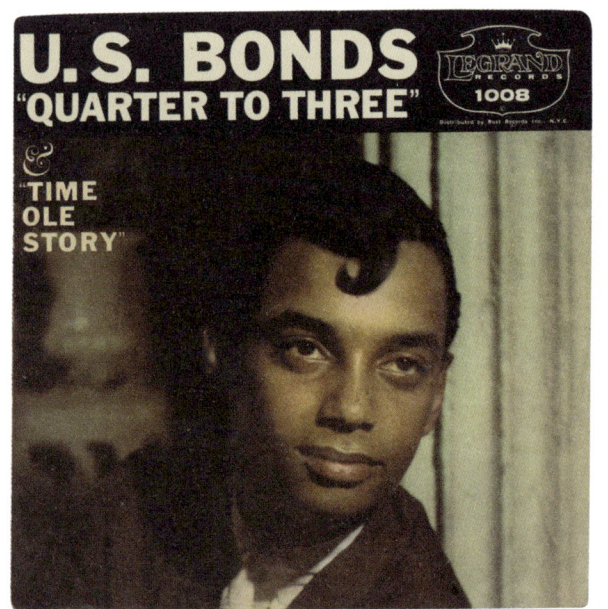
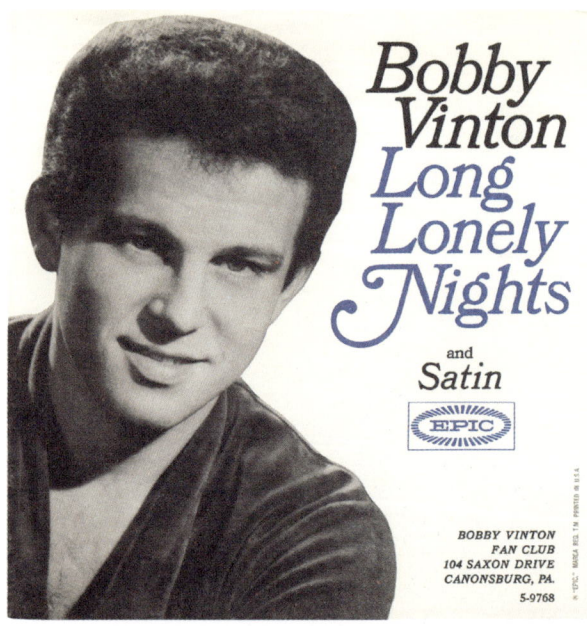
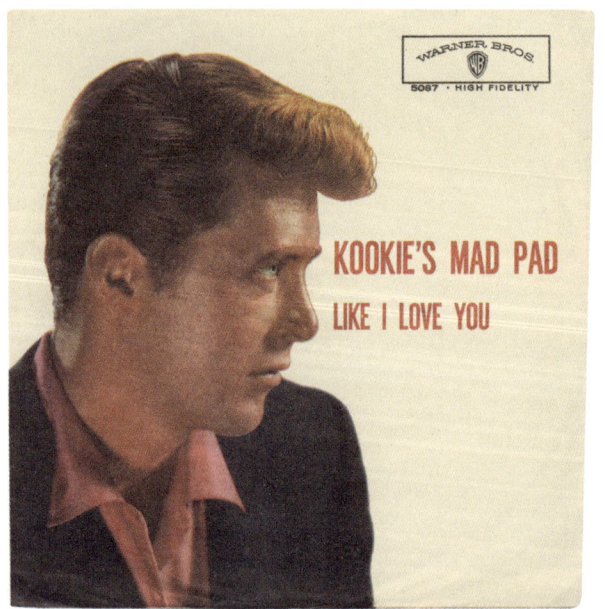
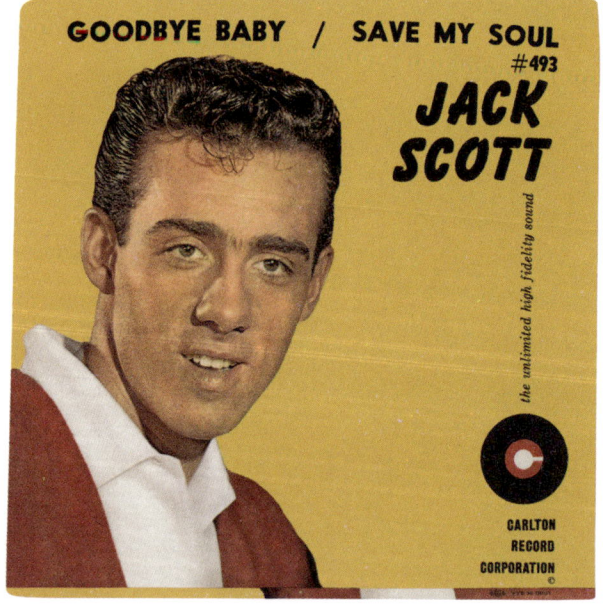

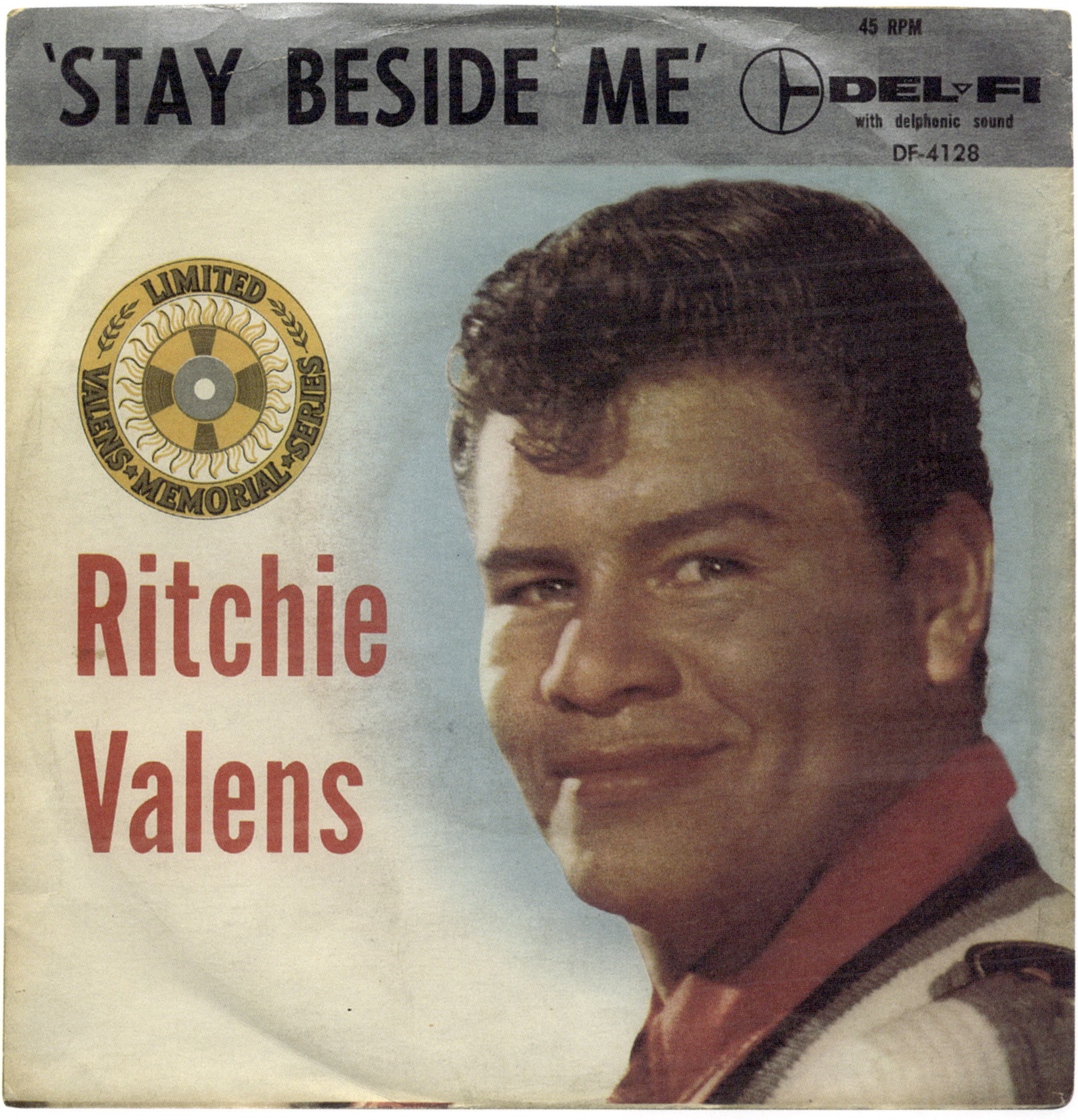

'STAY BESIDE ME'

DEL-FI
with delphonic sound

45 RPM
DF-4128

Ritchie Valens

STEREO 100 862-100

THE UNDERTONES

HERE COMES THE SUMMER

EAGLES

PLEASE COME HOME FOR CHRISTMAS
B/W FUNKY NEW YEAR

PRODUCED AND ENGINEERED BY BILL SZYMCZYK FOR PANDORA PRODUCTIONS LTD.

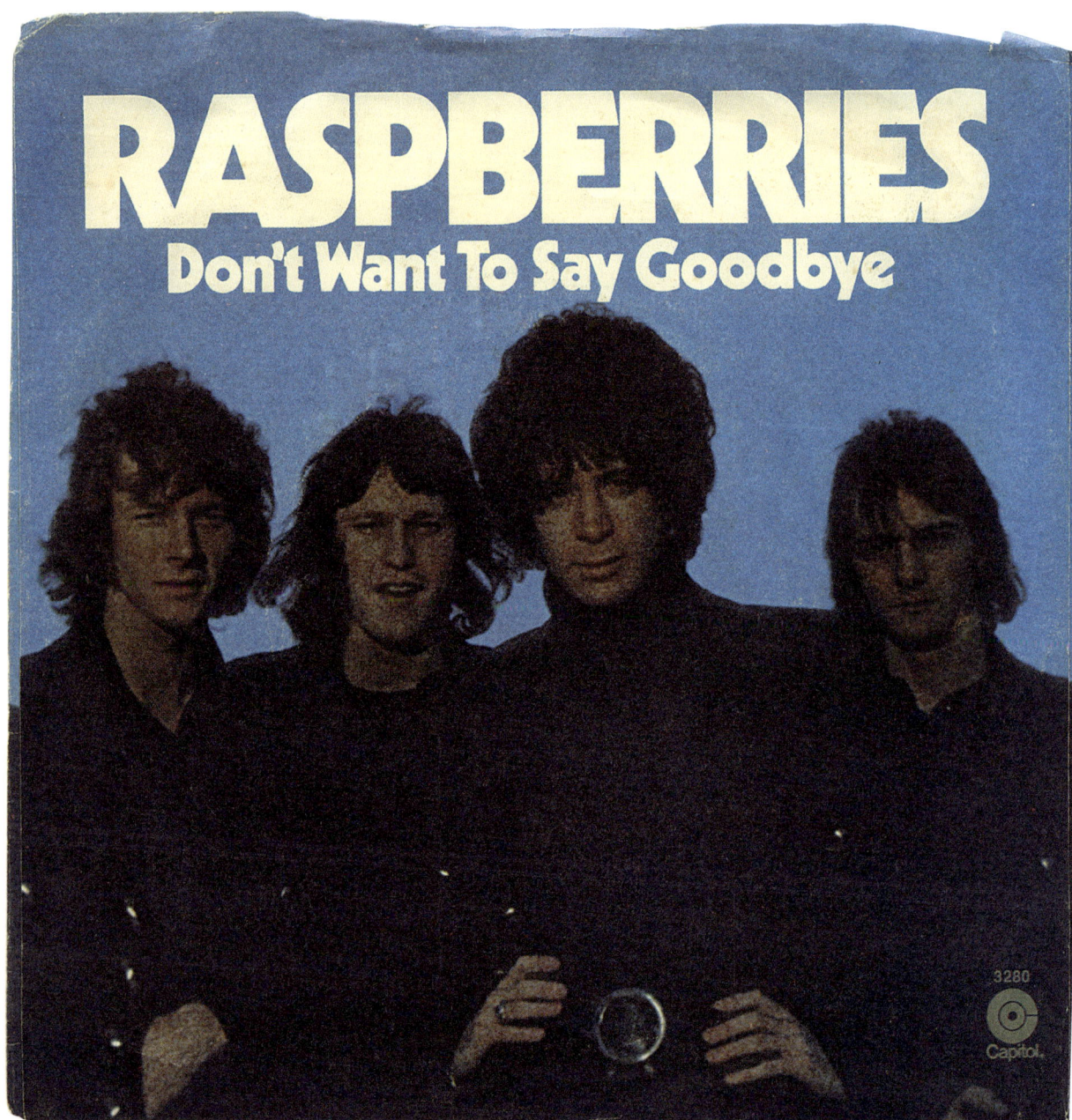

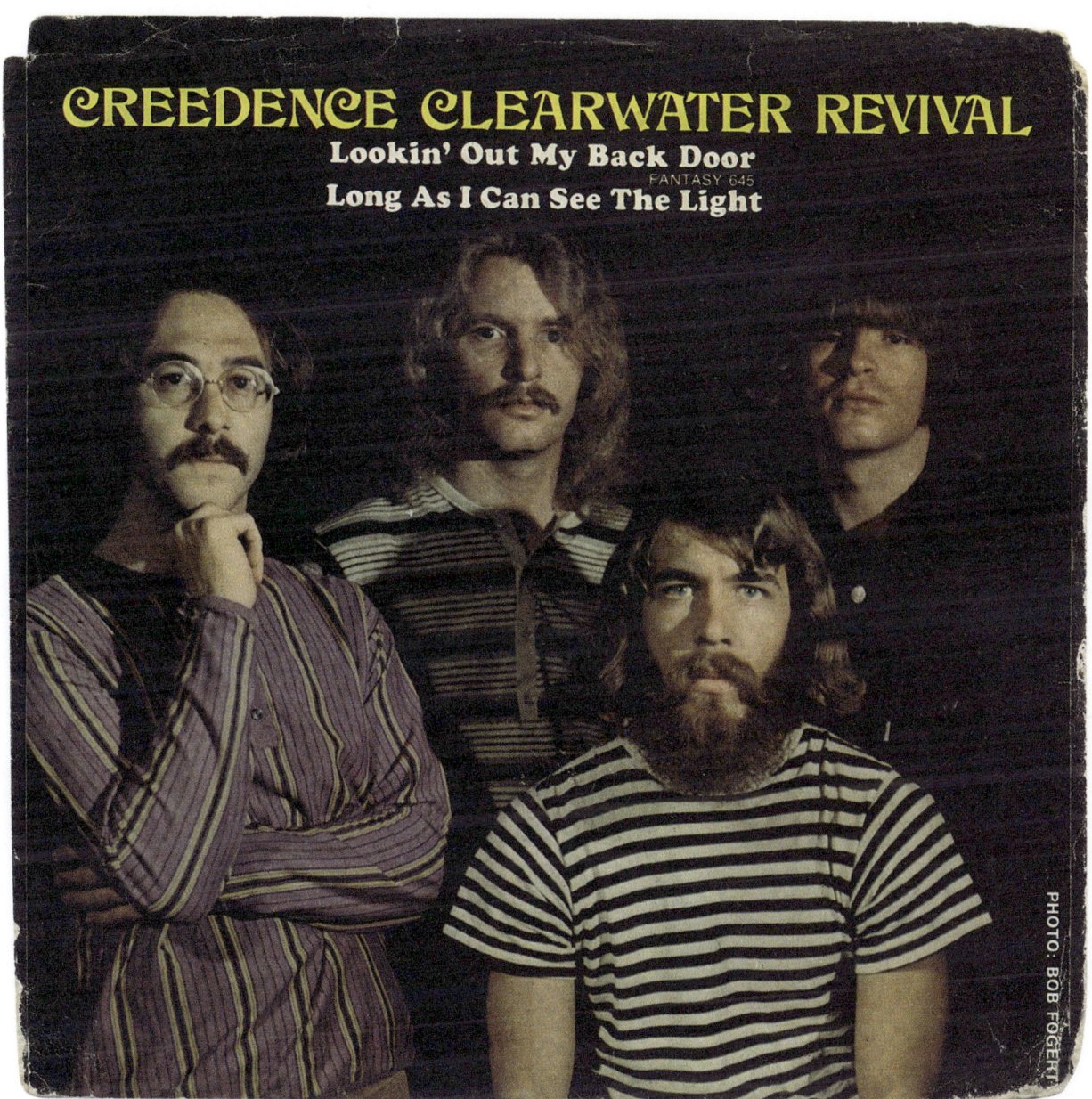

MY LITTLE TOWN
SIMON AND GARFUNKEL
PLUS
RAG DOLL
ART GARFUNKEL

YOU'RE KIND
PAUL SIMON

Photo: Edie Baskin

RATS INTO ROBOTS

1.) PRETEXT FOR WAR

YOUR LABORED SPEECH SOMEHOW CONVINCES A NOD TO GOD AND THE COUNTRY FOLLOWS. BUT THE COURSE HAS BEEN DECIDED. AND THEIR FATE HAS BEEN DECIDED. YOUR DECEPTIONS AND MISDIRECTIONS CANNOT CONCEAL A DECADES OLD PLAN TO SEIZE AND DOMINATE IN THE INTEREST OF POWER AND GREED. YOUR WORDS ARE NOTHING BUT LIES BUILT ON MISCONCEPTIONS THAT SERVE ONLY AS PRETEXTS FOR WAR.

EARLIER THIS YEAR THE BUSH ADMINISTRATION, LEAD BY NEO-CONSERVATIVE WAR HAWKS LIKE HIMSELF, MANAGED TO CONVINCE THE AMERICAN PEOPLE THAT A WAR AGAINST THE COUNTRY WAS PUMPED UP. LINKS TO TERRORISTS WERE MANUFACTURED, AND A PLEA WAS MADE FOR THE HISTORICALLY WE HELPED KEEP IN POWER. IT'S NOT DIFFICULT TO UNDERSTAND WHY CAREER BE AFTER ONE OF THE RICHEST OIL REGIONS IN THE WORLD. IN FACT THEY'VE BEEN ATTEMPTING ENERGY CRISIS OF THE 1970'S. WHAT IS ASTONISHING IS THE WILLINGNESS OF THE AMERICAN DESPITE KNOWING THE OBVIOUS BENEFITS THAT WILL BE REAPED BY CABINET MEMBERS WITH THOUSANDS OF INNOCENT LIVES WOULD BE LOST NOT ONLY IN THE WAR WE MAKE ON THE AND DISORDER THAT WOULD FOLLOW. DESPITE ACKNOWLEDGING THAT GROWING ANTI-AMERICAN AGAINST OUR COUNTRY, THE AMERICAN PEOPLE WERE WILLING AND EAGER TO FOLLOW THE CAN'T UNDERSTAND. AS OF THIS WRITING, ABSOLUTELY NO WEAPONS OF MASS DESTRUCTION LEGITIMATE TIES HAVE BEEN FOUND BETWEEN SADDAM HUSSEIN'S REGIME AND AL QAEDA, CERTAINLY NOT WELCOMED THEIR "LIBERATORS." IT IS CRUCIAL NOW MORE THAN EVER THE INTERNATIONAL SOLIDARITY MOVEMENT AND CONTINUE TO FIGHT FOR PEACE WORLD. -ADAM R.

DONALD RUMSFELD, PAUL WOLFOWITZ, DICK CHENEY, AND W. OF IRAQ WAS IN THEIR BEST INTEREST. THE THREAT OF WMD'S FREEDOM OF THE IRAQI PEOPLE FROM A REGIME WHICH OILMEN, LIKE THOSE IN THE BUSH ADMINISTRATION, WOULD TO CONTROL THE OIL FIELDS OF THE PERSIAN GULF SINCE THE PEOPLE TO FOLLOW SUCH A DECEITFUL AND DEADLY ROAD, TIES TO THE OIL INDUSTRY, DESPITE REALIZING THAT PEOPLE OF IRAQ BUT ALSO IN THE ENSUING CHAOS SENTIMENT ONLY LEADS TO MORE TERRORISM PRESIDENT TO WAR. THAT IS WHAT I HAVE BEEN FOUND IN IRAQ, NO AND THE IRAQI PEOPLE HAVE THAT WE SUPPORT AND JUSTICE IN THE

2.) FROZE IN A MAZE

WE FEAST IN THE BEAST WHERE EVERYTHING LIES WAITING FOR. US. A PROCESS THAT IS NEVER ENDING. WE LAY THE TRAIL OF CRUMBS, BUT NEVER FIND OUR WAY OUT. AND WHEN WE LOOK BACK ITS ALL A LIVING HELL.

DEFINITION:

ACTION...LEARN... REACTION

RATS INTO ROBOTS WOULD LIKE TO THANK: ALL OF OUR FRIENDS AND FAMILY FOR THEIR SUPPORT. BRENT EYESTONE, DAN WILBURN, TEXTBOOK TRAITORS, FUNERAL DINER, FUNERAL FOR ROSEWATER THE DEAD HATE THE LIVING, JENNIFER NEWTON (PRACTICE SPACE EXTRAORDINAIRE), AND ANYONE WHO HAS EVER HELPED US OUT IN ANY WAY. WE THANK YOU!

ALL MUSIC BY RATS INTO ROBOTS. THIS RECORDING WAS ENGINEERED BY DAN WILBURN AT WORKBOOK STUDIOS, COLUMBUS, OH BETWEEN THE DATES OF 5/20/03-6/21/03. ORIGINAL PHOTO BY ADAM LOWE. INSIDE LABEL ART BY RYAN WHALEN. LAYOUT/DESIGN BY BRENT EYESTONE. RATS INTO ROBOTS IS: ADAM, RYAN, ADAM. MAGIC BULLET SUPPORTS THE POLITICAL OPINIONS OF ITS BANDS. MAIL: RATS INTO ROBOTS 947 MELROSE BLVD. PICKERINGTON, OH 43147 USA WEBSITE: WWW.RATSINTOROBOTS.COM, FOR BOOKING OR QUESTIONS: EAGLESORES@AOL.COM

C&P 2003 THE MAGIC BULLET RECORD CO. PO BOX 2370 MERRIFIELD, VA 22116 USA THIS IS MAGIC BULLET #48. SUPPORT INDEPENDENT MEDIA, MUSIC, THOUGHT. THANK YOU WWW.MAGICBULLETRECORDS.COM INFO@MAGICBULLETRECORDS.COM

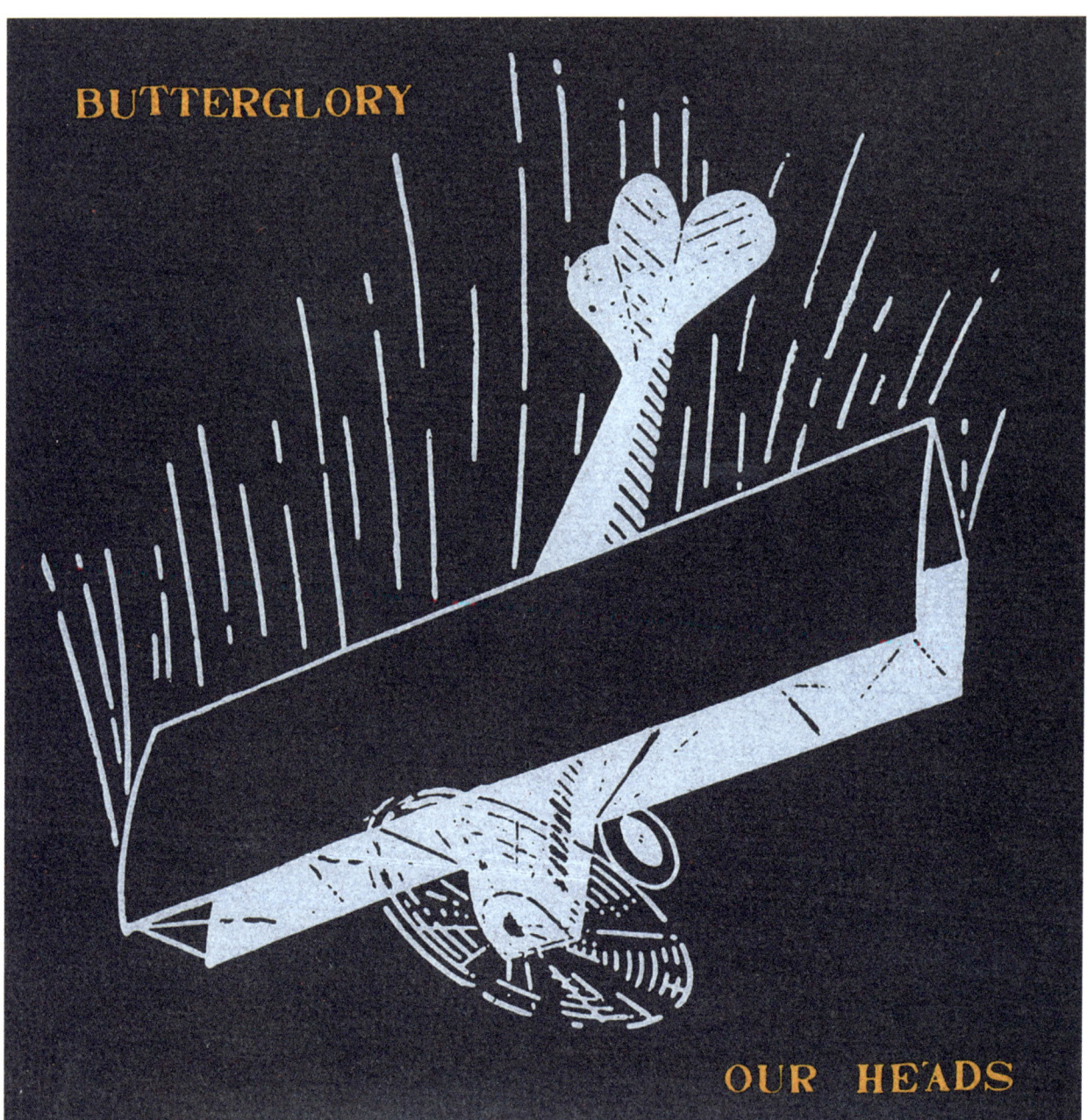

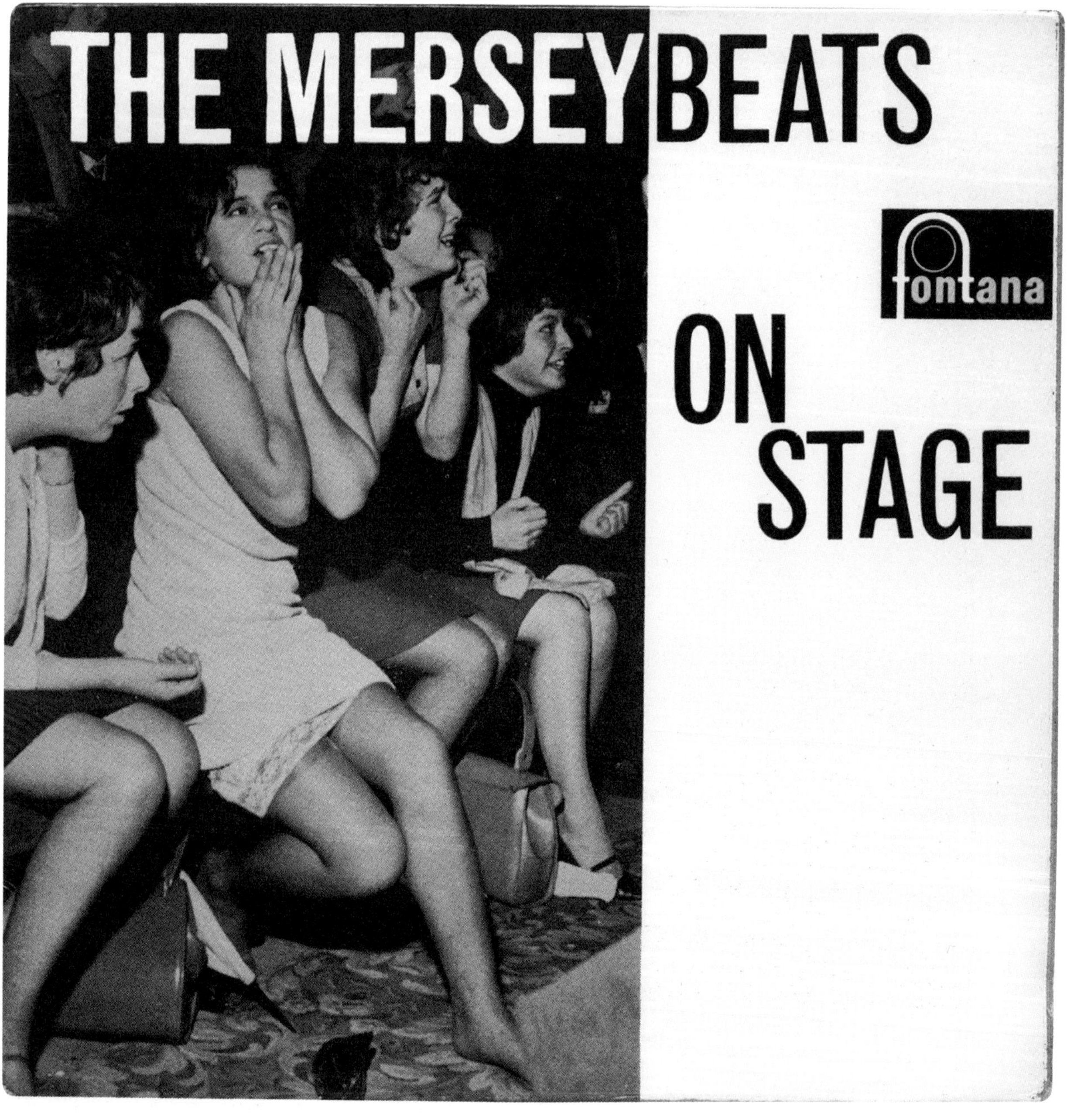

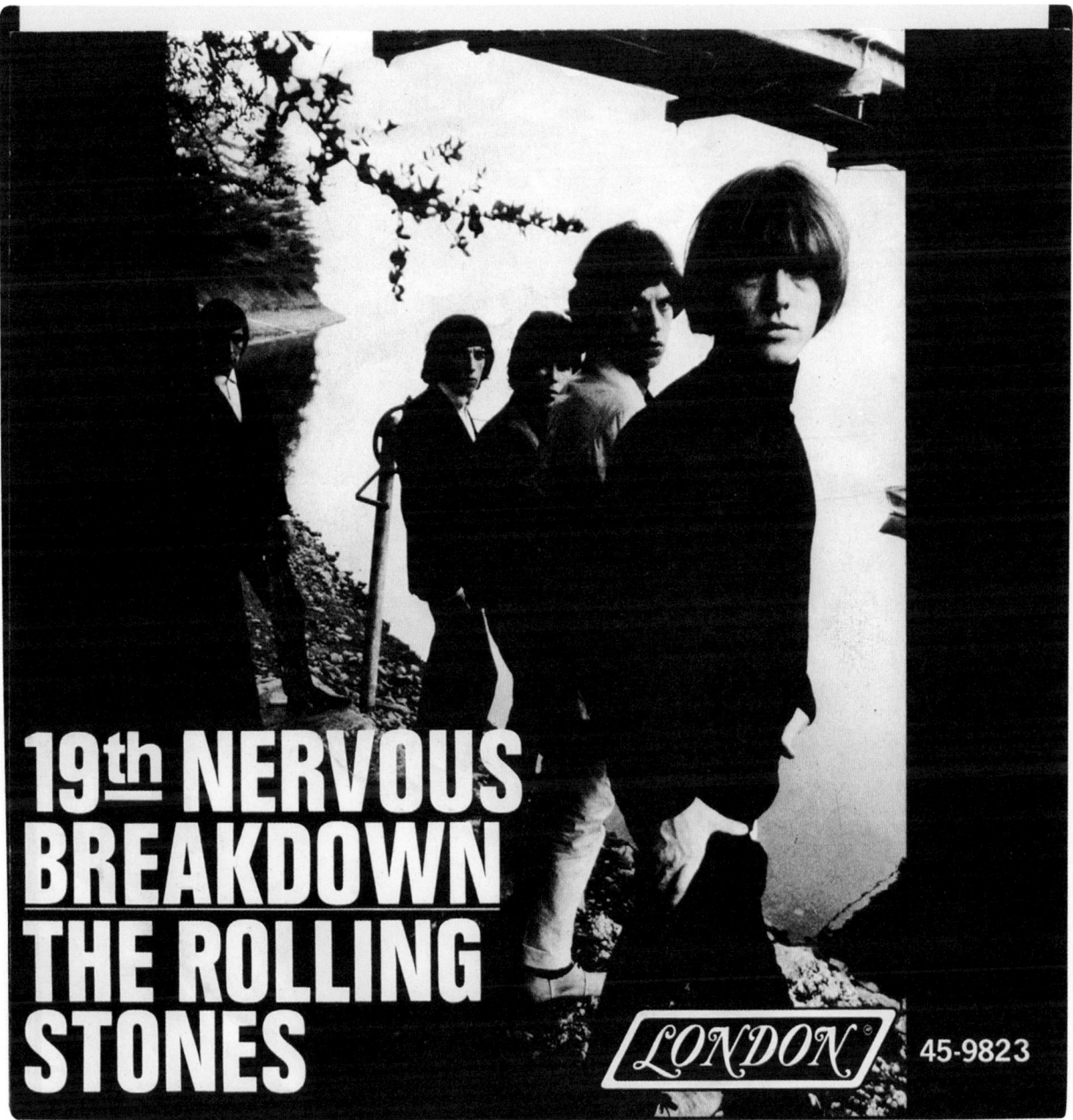

Steve Forbert
"ARRIVING LIVE"

NEMPEROR RECORDS DEMONSTRATION/NOT FOR SALE

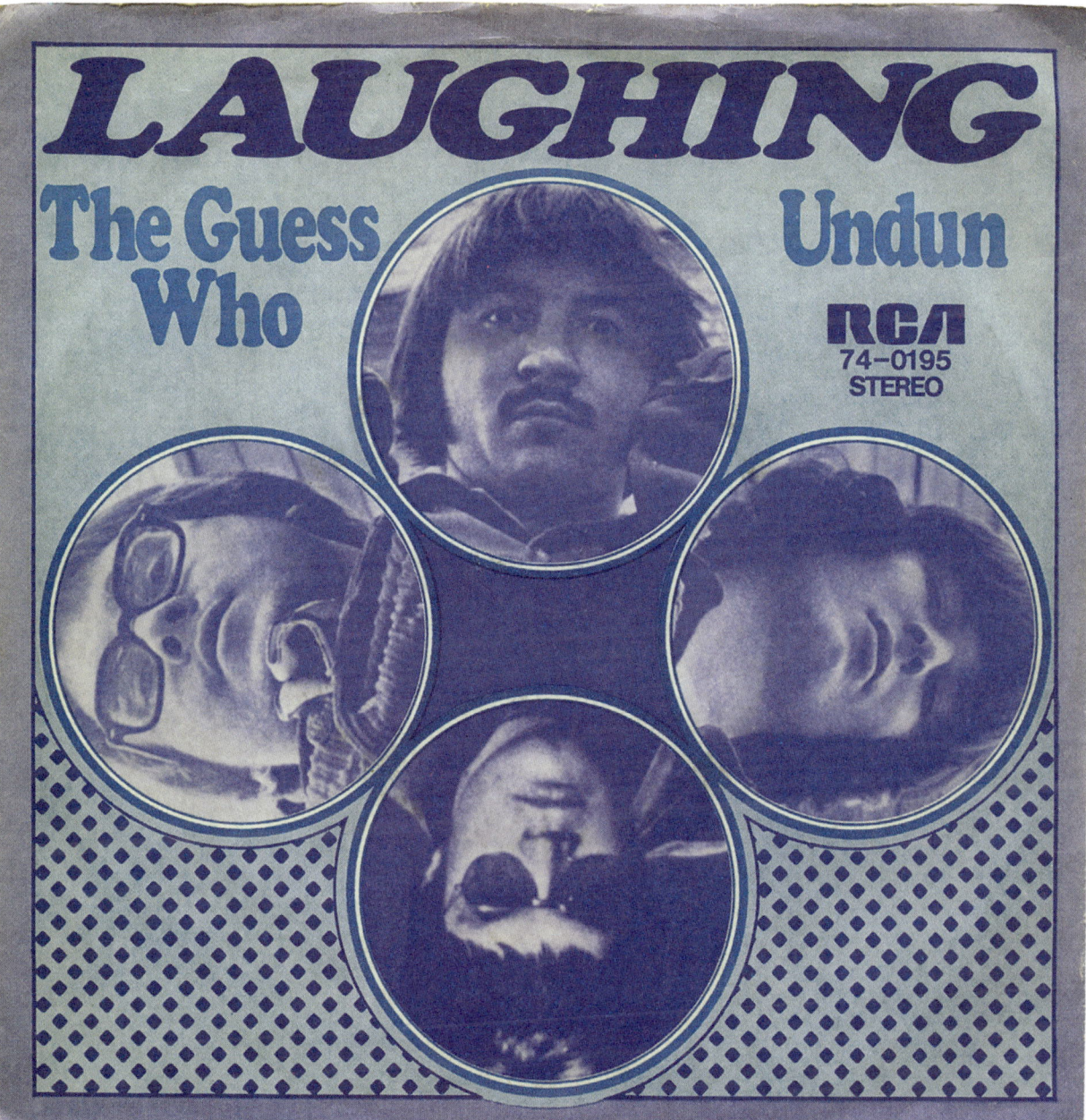

O SUPERMAN

EP 33

LAURIE ANDERSON

フローダス / アトミック ファイヤーボール
FRODUS / ATOMIC FIREBALL

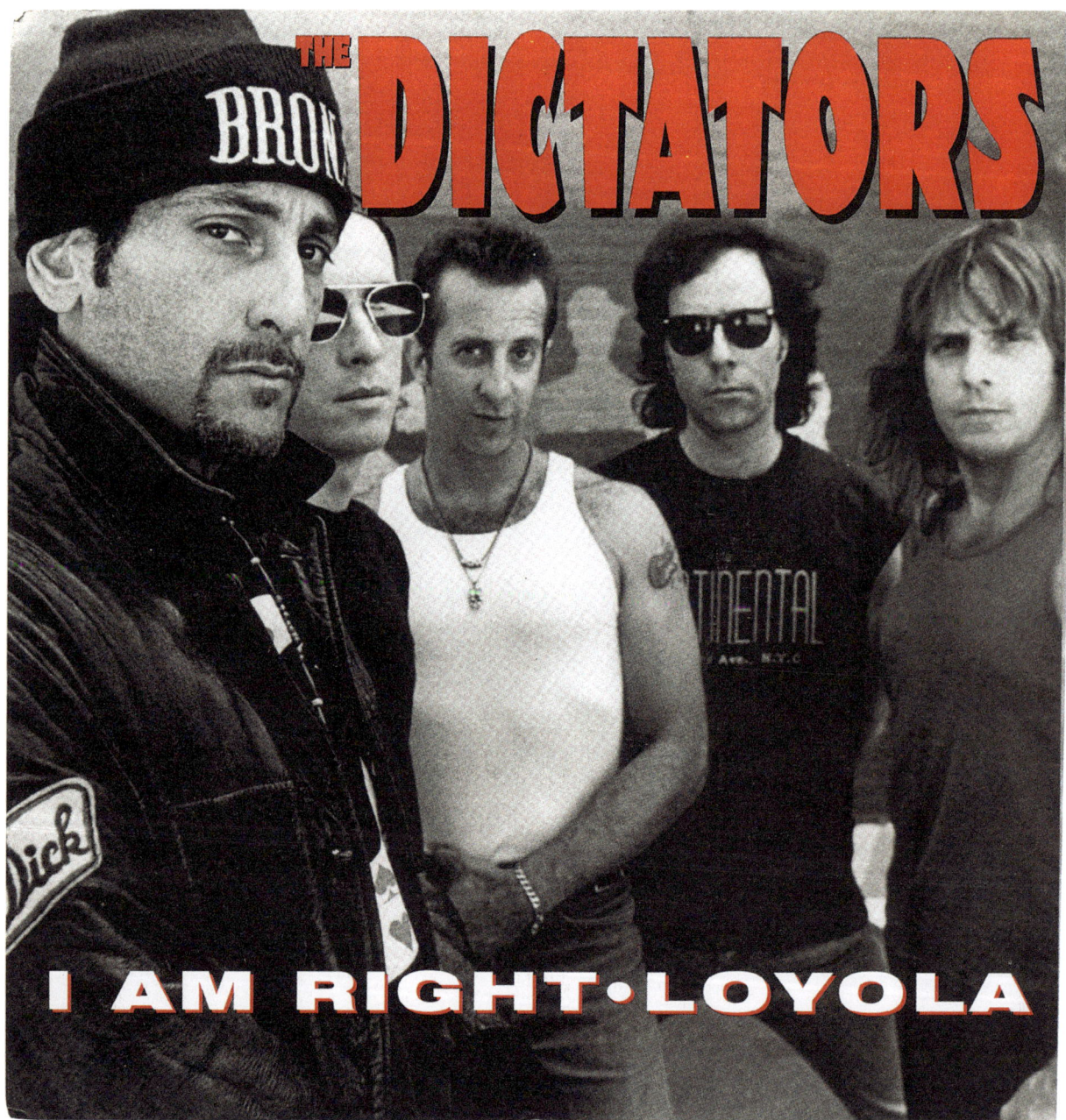

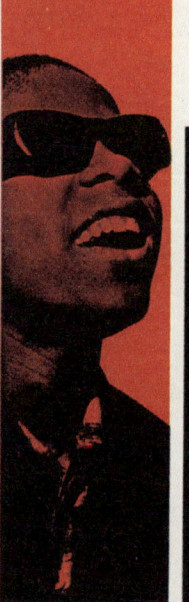

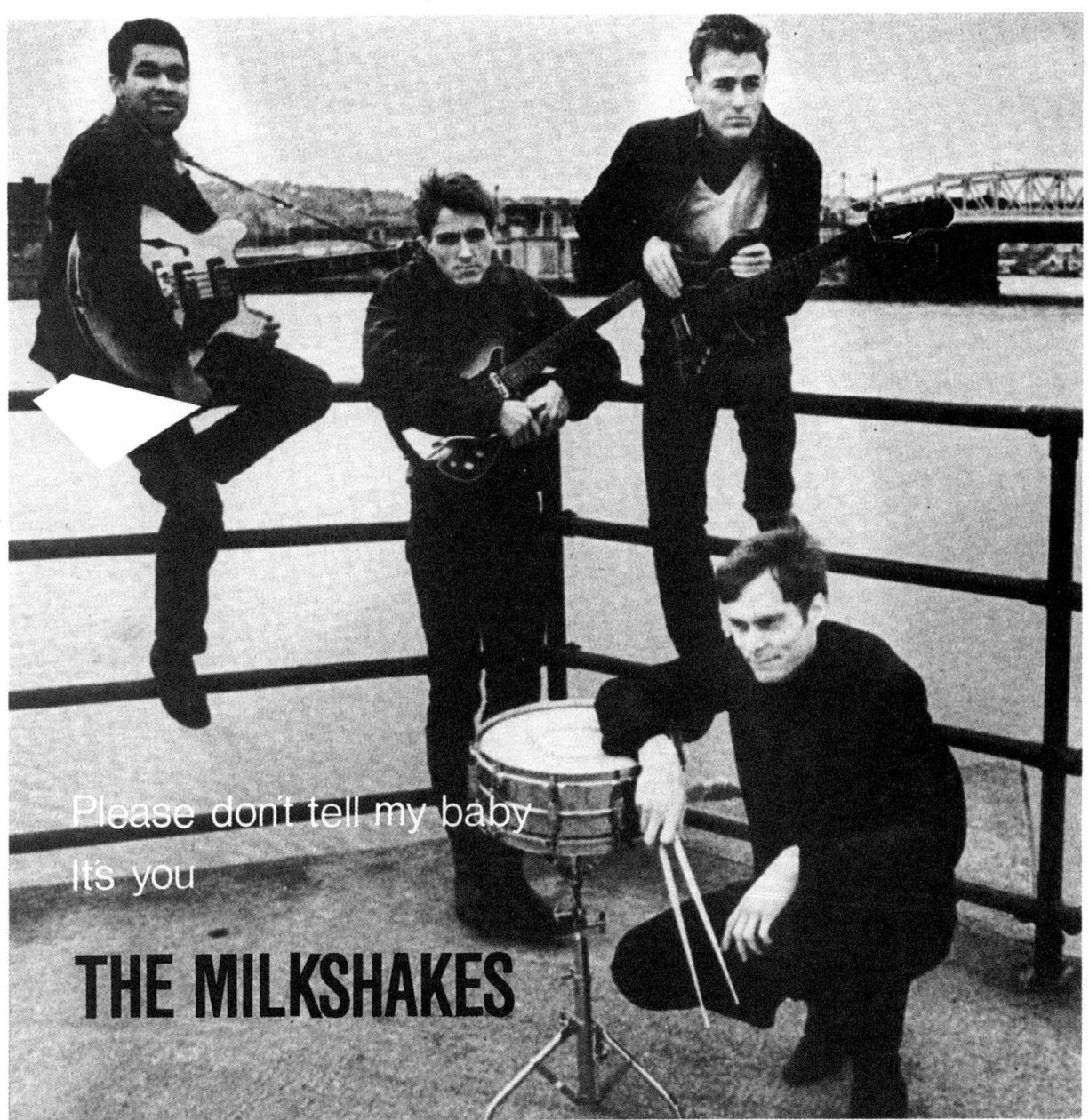

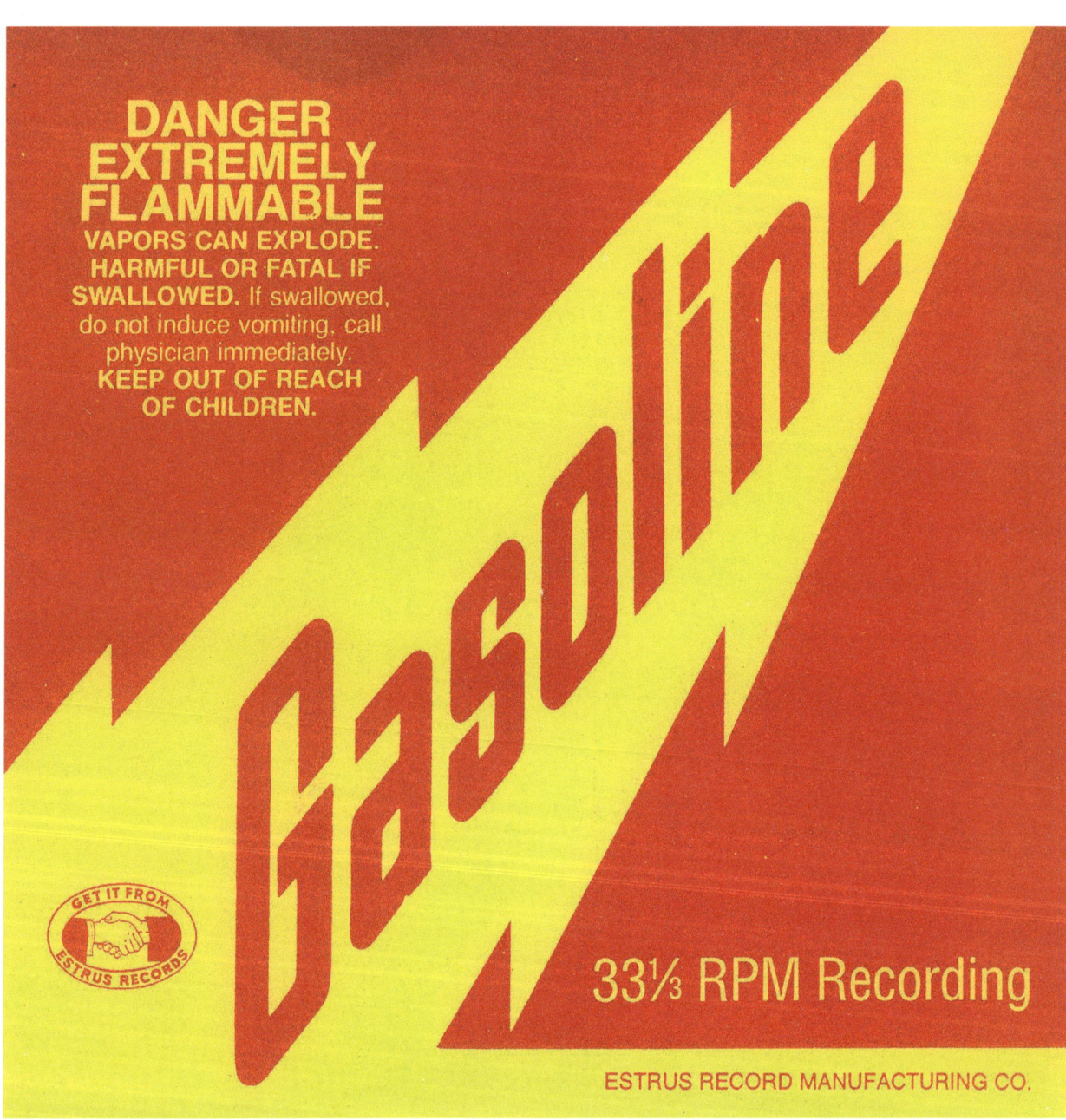

RAMONES
Don't Come Close

JAD FAIR

MY baby

THE PRETENDERS

TOM HAZELMYER

Alright, uninformed one, it goes like this: In the prehistoric dark days before Internet downloads, cable television, and, hell, even before the compact disc, there was vinyl. It came in a bunch of shapes and colors, but it pretty much boiled down to two sizes: 7-inch (single) and 12-inch (LP). I will spare you the details on the mechanics of dragging a needle across a hunk of plastic to make sound, but what I will harp on was its importance. Until the 1980s, there was little mainstream media that focused on rock music. With only four television networks, a handful of nationally distributed rock magazines, and likely just one or two rock radio stations in most markets (all controlled by major labels, therefore locking out underground and local talent), the alternatives were few and far between. The unceasing bleakness is near impossible to explain to those generations that have access to unlimited communication. At that time your only insight into what was happening in New York, London, L.A., Chicago, etc., was likely through 7-inch slabs of vinyl.

Being trapped in the stone-age scenario I've laid out (even the music video was in its infancy in the late '70s) resulted in barely any visuals to associate with the music of this movement. Your entire impression of a band was likely derived from what packaging might be wrapped around the record and the sound you heard after you dropped the needle. This partly explains why such care was placed on a lot of those sleeves. It wasn't just another facet of a musician's image; it was likely the only public image that could be created.

The U.K. punk/post-punk late-70s scene was my entry point to the 7-inch single. Not only was it a more affordable means for checking out a band (versus laying out three hours' wages on an LP), but the extreme style and cutting-edge art and packaging was worlds beyond the bare papered sleeved singles common to American major label releases. These were musical explosions that in a lot of cases were draped in art every bit as incendiary as the tunes themselves. From the blisteringly raw Jamie Reid Sex Pistols singles art to the austere Joy Division "Love Will Tear Us Apart" single, and all points in between, the graphics coming from the U.K. weren't just an afterthought to the music. They were a flag. They were an art form. This visual/musical onslaught was comprised of varied singles, which shared one thing: they looked like nothing else out there. Neither Madison Avenue nor any part of the mainstream culture had tapped that Punk Look. It was a secret Masonic handshake for entry into an exclusive underground world. I clearly remember plunking down cash for "War Dance," a single by a new band called Killing Joke, for the sole reason that I loved the sleeve art, only to have my head sheared off

 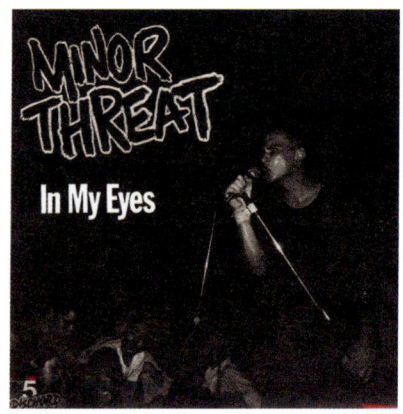

by the music contained within. This happened frequently. I was not alone in this respect.

At the dawn of the '80s, when it was our turn to pick up guitars, we took a lot of the influences from the '75–'77 U.K. and New York City scenes, but our sound morphed it into something more uniquely American. It was harder, faster, and never accessible. It was called hardcore. Unlike in the U.K., in America this moment in music reached outside of its small cloistered fan base only years after it started. We had all been weaned on singles, and they were the chosen format for this movement. Though influenced by the previous punk aesthetics, there were a few new twists. For starters, unlike in the U.K., where there was some major label and healthy independent label money to help the design along, in the United States it was almost entirely do-it-yourself. So you had Stretch Marks in Winnipeg, or Die Kreuzen in Milwaukee, or Husker Dü in Minneapolis, or Black Flag in L.A. doing singles on their own. The graphics at that point were as raw and immediate as hardcore itself. Cheap and accessible, Xeroxing and rub-off lettering were the easiest means at hand, and resulted in a graphic sensibility that's still tapped into today. This rough, hand-made aesthetic became the standard for hardcore sleeves: worn like a uniform, this look ultimately became a cliché, so that anyone viewing it had a pretty clear indication of what was being offered inside.

By the mid-'80s however, the single seemed slated for irrelevance yet again, as the advent of cassettes offered unknown bands an even cheaper method to get the music out there. Also, a slew of Indie labels—SST, Dischord, Touch & Go, Homestead, and others—were able to start producing LPs. 7-inch records had seemingly lost steam and the popularity gained from the previous punk and hardcore explosions. Some groups stayed true to the 7-inch record, wearing it as a badge of a "real" band—these same groups were also written about in DIY fanzines, which were hugely popular in the late '80s and early '90s, and played on the more adventuresome college radio of the same era. The same factors that brought the single back to underground prominence existed in full effect, and new emerging labels such as Sub Pop, Sympathy For The Record Industry, Amphetamine Reptile, and many others helped extend the life of the 7-inch record. Most of the players at that time understood the impact a single could have and ran with it. Drag into the mix the many artists and designers of sleeve art, which would go on to fame in the art world. Where it will go from there? Could not really tell you, but I find myself sitting at the table stuffing small editions to this day—I'm hooked.

THESE WERE MUSICAL EXPLOSIONS THAT IN A LOT OF CASES WERE DRAPED IN ART EVERY BIT AS INCENDIARY AS THE TUNES THEMSELVES.

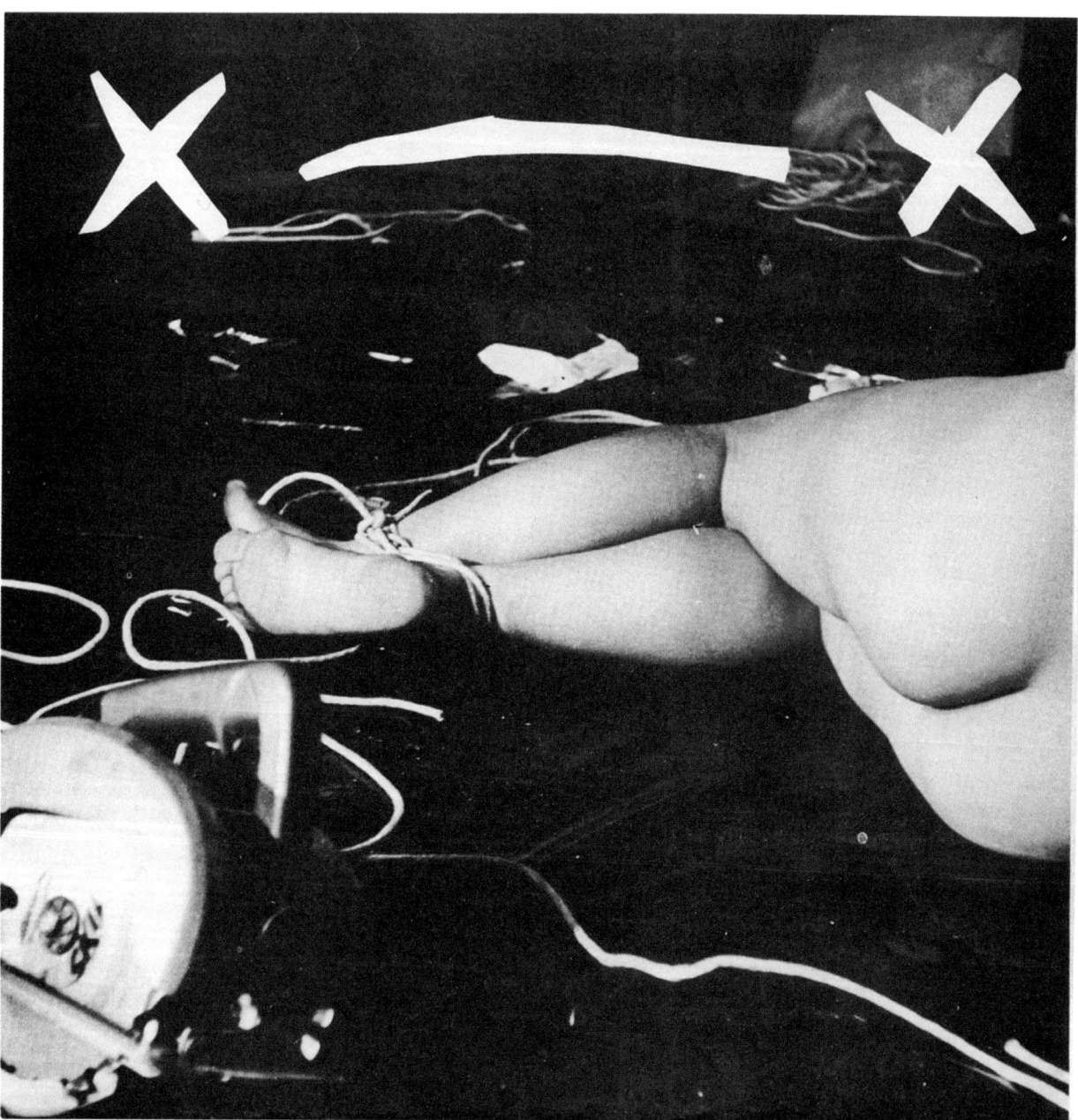

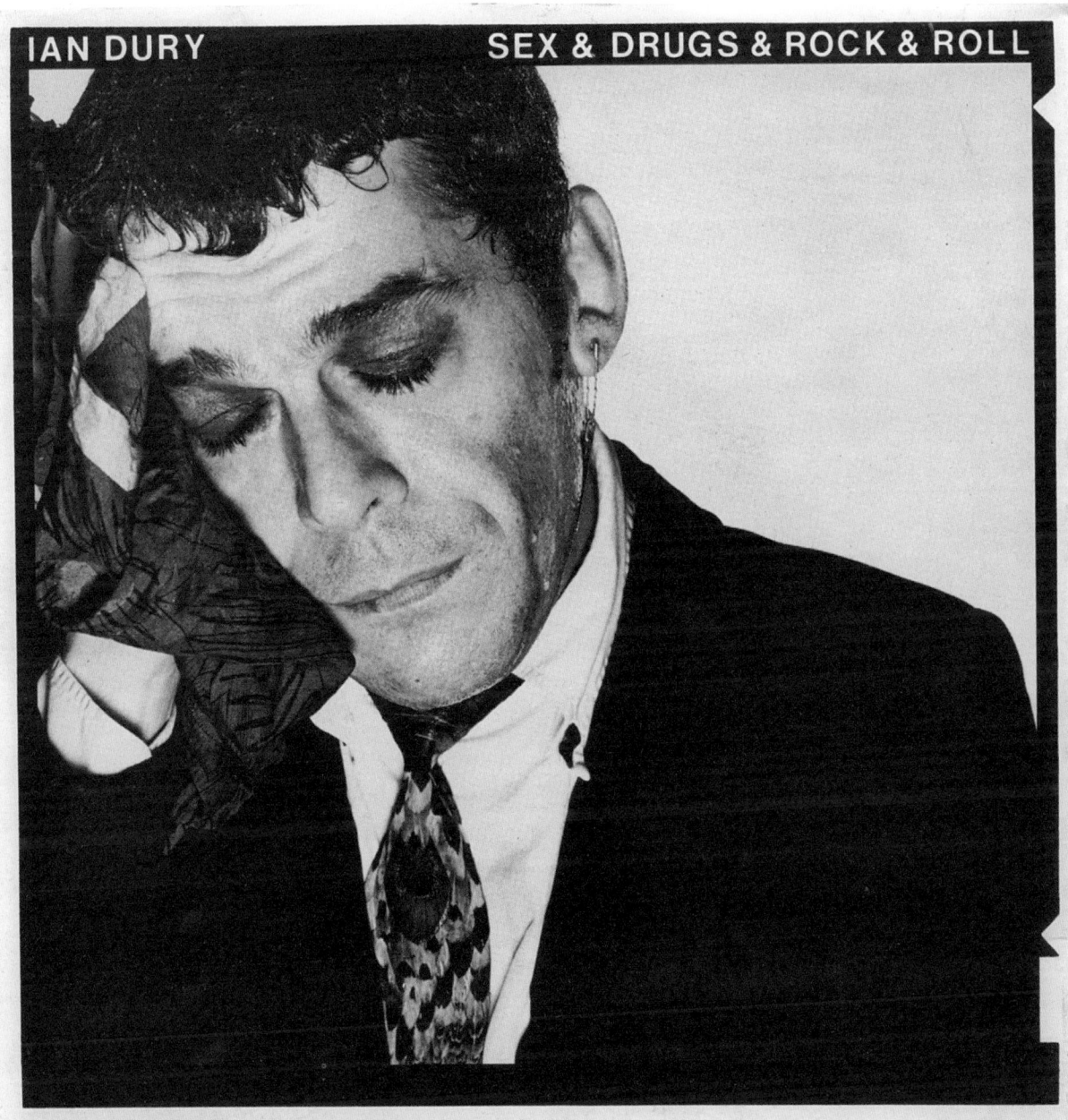

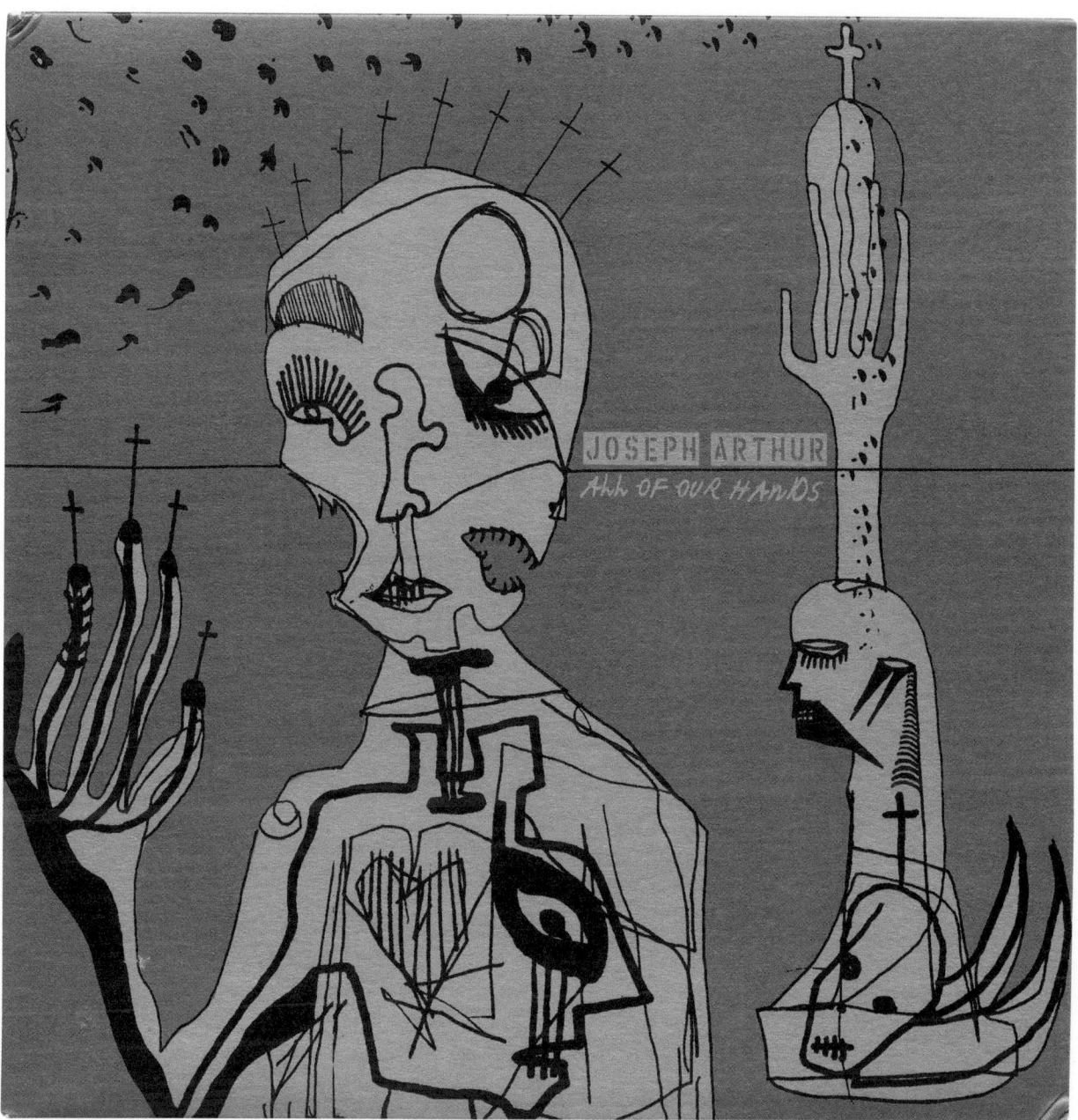

DOPE-GUNS'N-FUCKING IN THE STREETS

VOLUME TWO

GOD BULLIES TAR HELIOS CREED LONELY MOANS

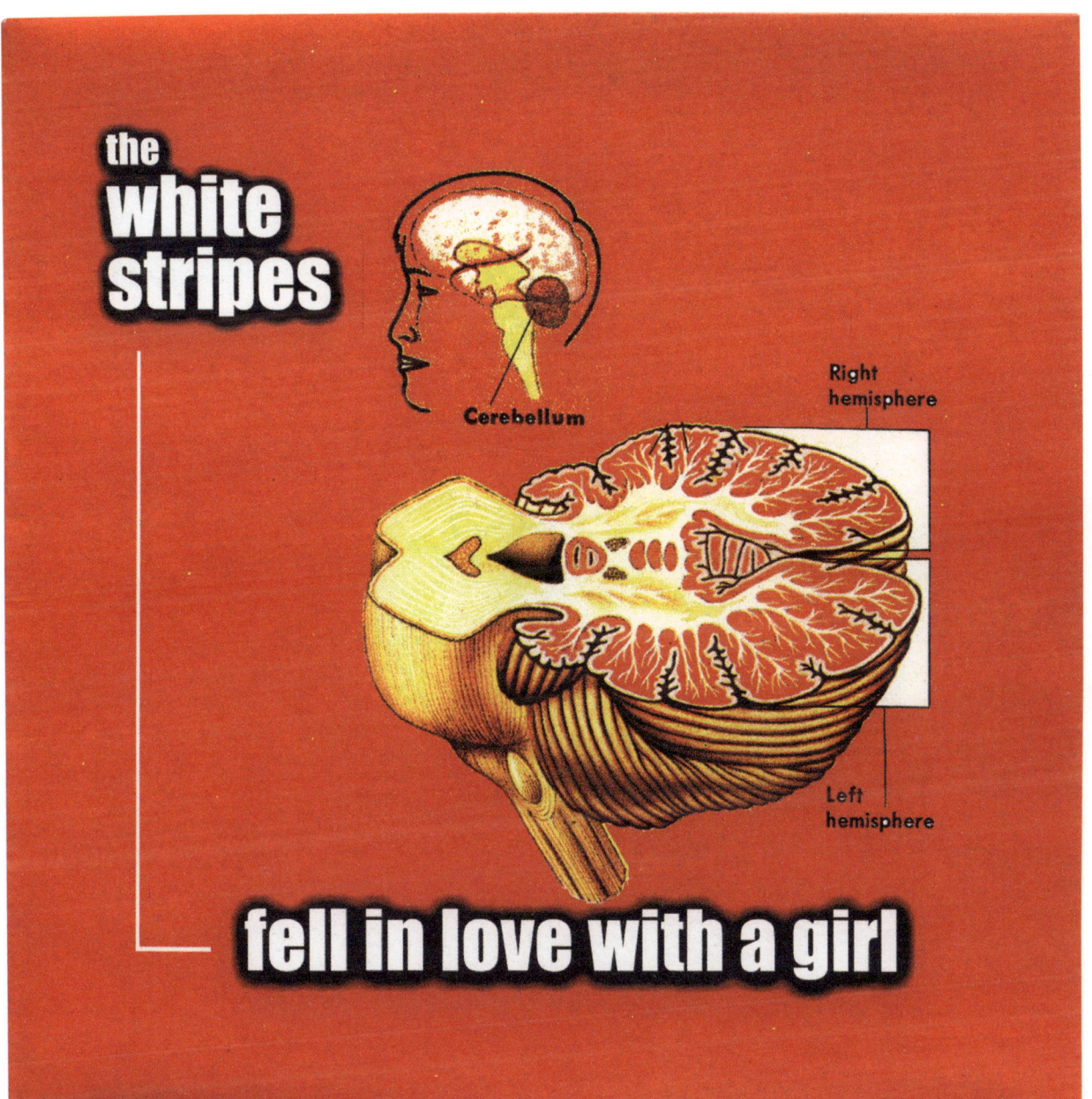

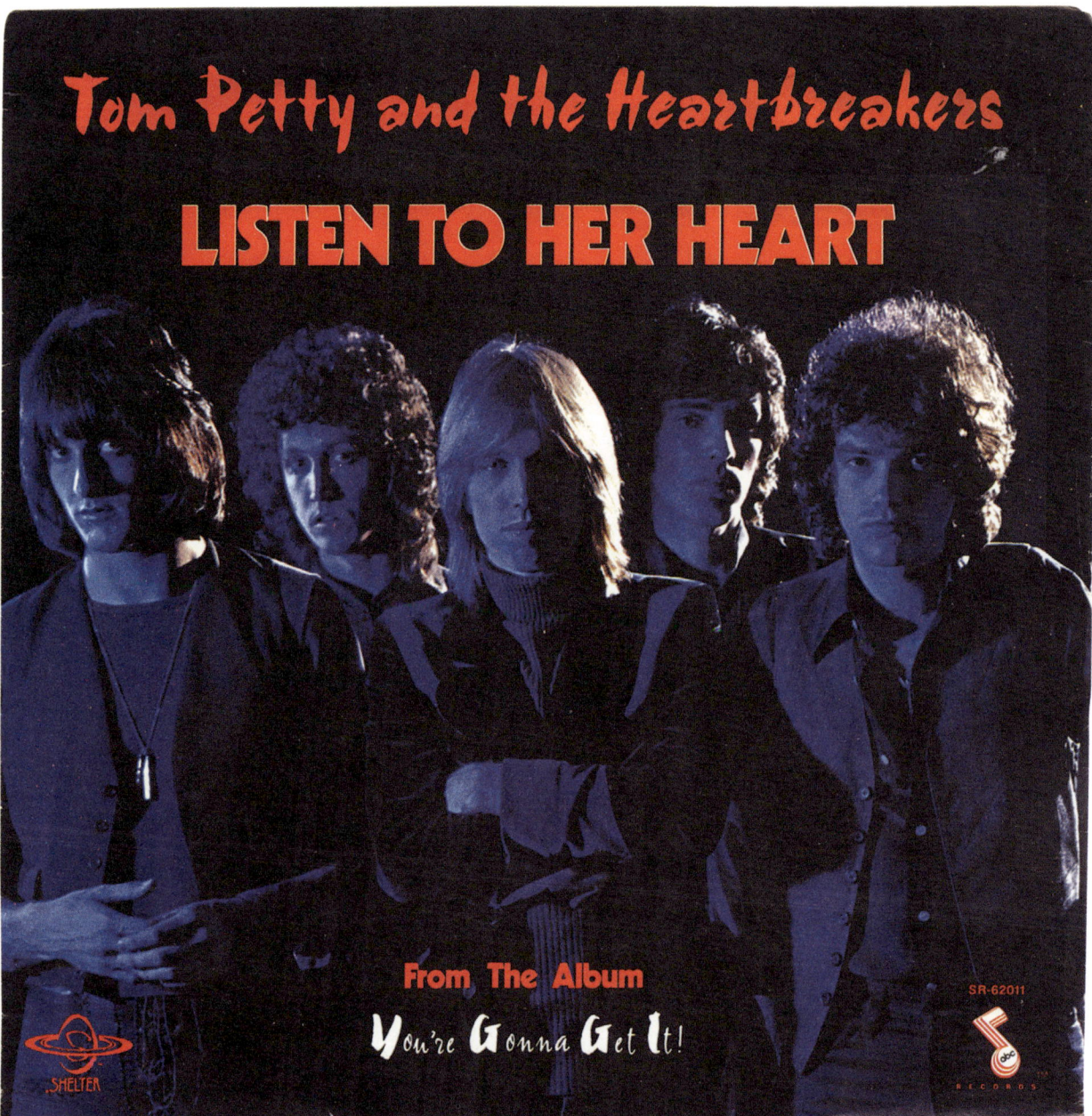

KINKS

EXTENDED PLAY

WATERLOO SUNSET
DAVID WATTS   A WELL RESPECTED MAN   STOP YOUR SOBBIN'

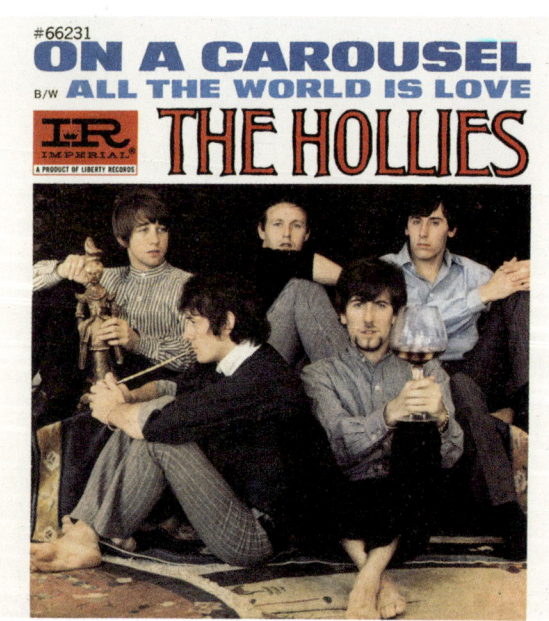

NOVA

WOMAN IS THE NIGGER OF THE WORLD

JOHN LENNON/PLASTIC ONO BAND

with Elephant's Memory and Invisible Strings

Apple 1848

SHE: "WOMAN IS THE NIGGER OF THE WORLD..."
MARCH 1969 THREE SHILLINGS AND SIXPENCE

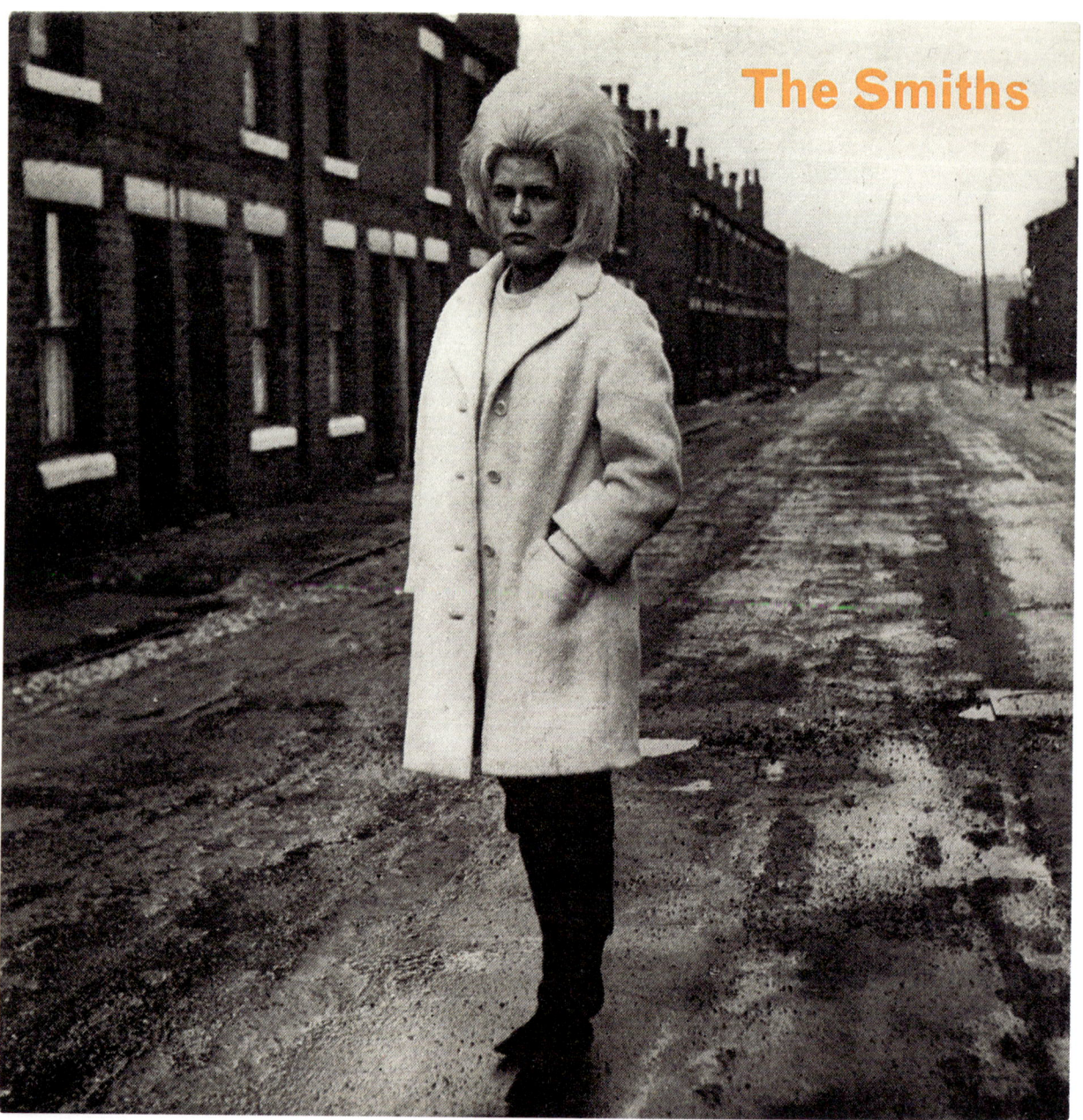

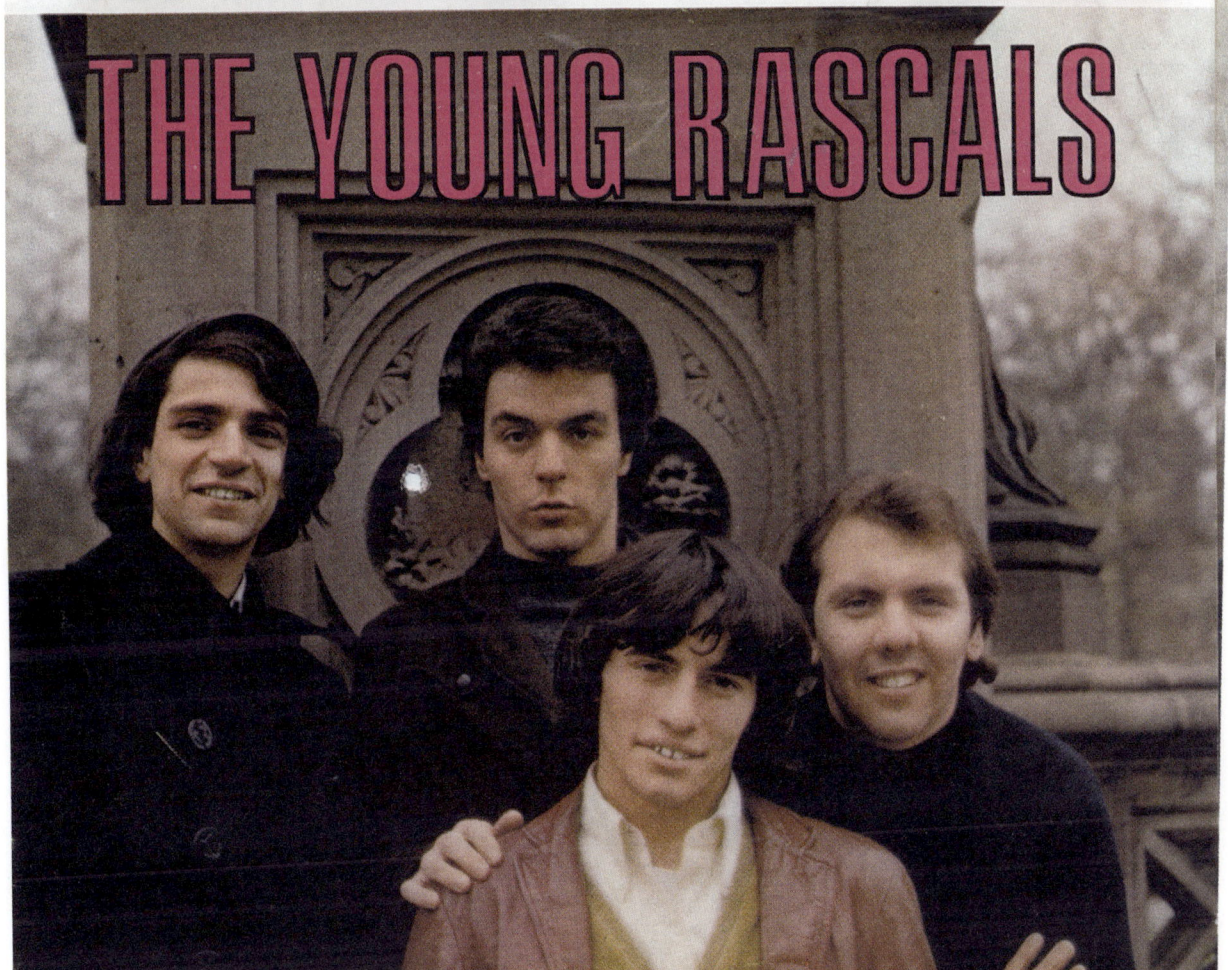

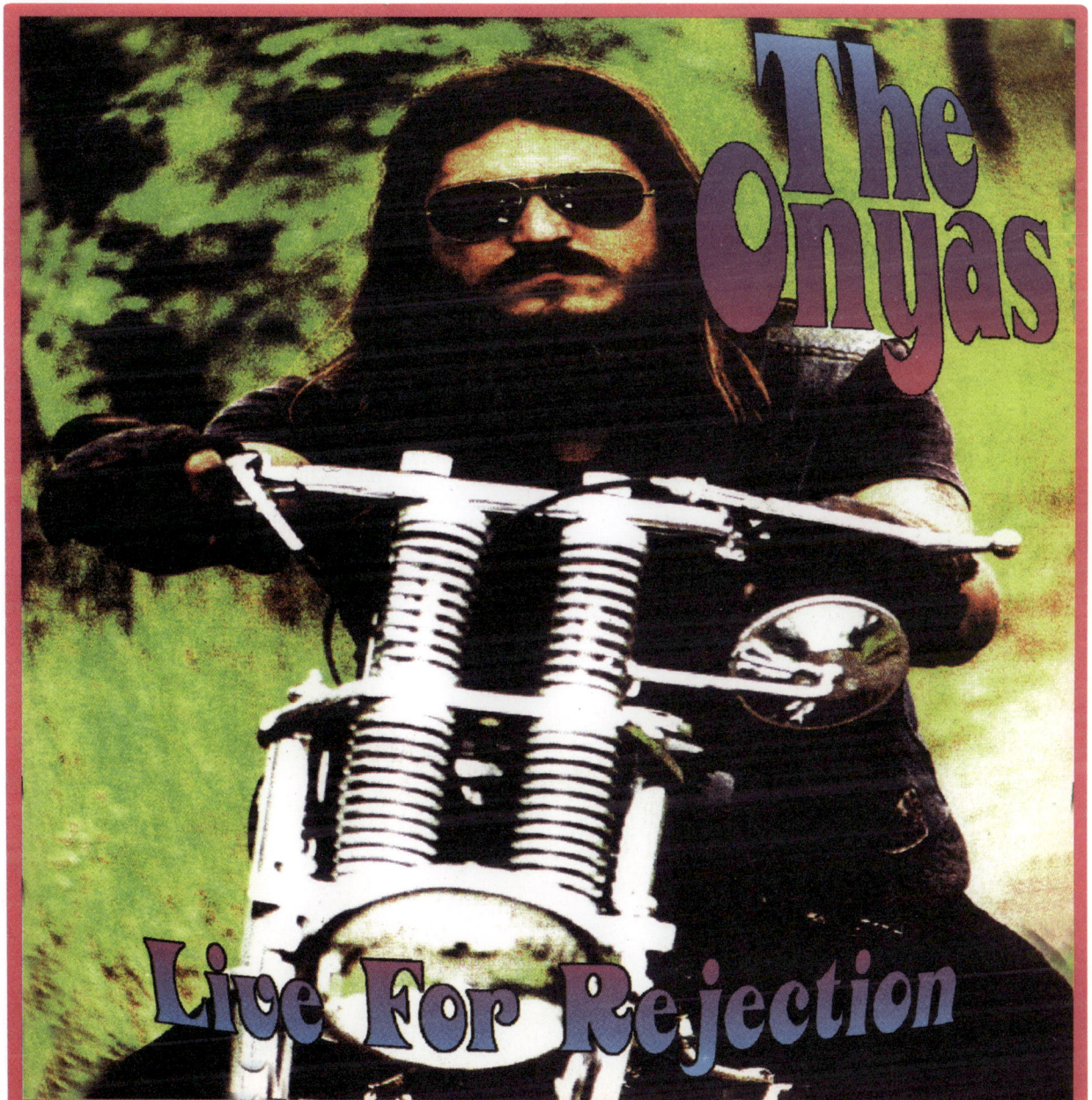

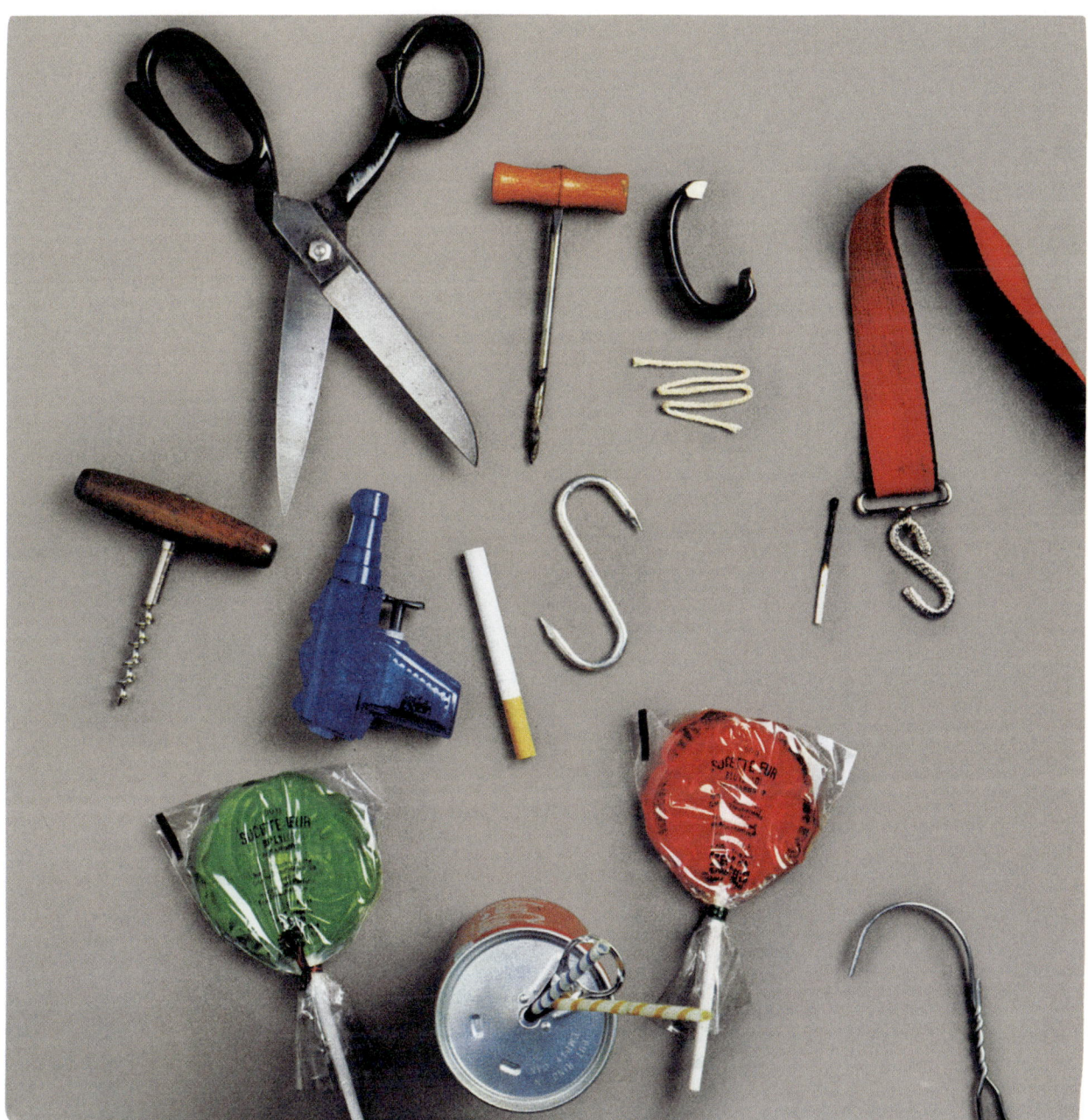

be your own PET

THIS MACHINE KILLS   JR EWING

ISA RWAY

SPLIT RECORDING

Q AND NOT U
HOT AND INFORMED
and the washington monument blinks goodnight
busy lights busy carpet
kiss distinctly american

Stealing Cars　　　　　　　　　　　　　　　　　　　**Bob Beland**

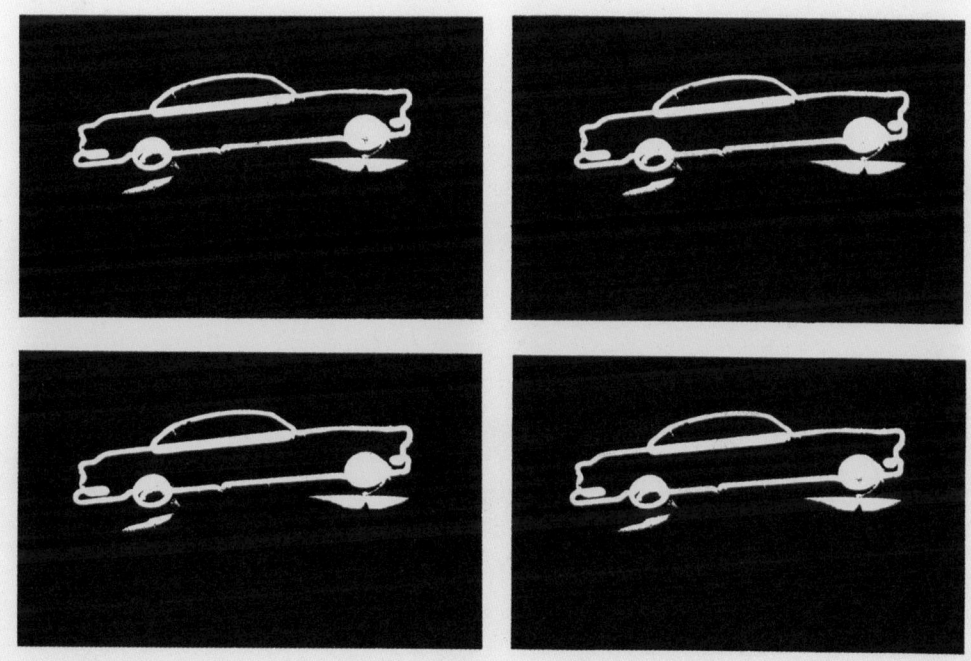

Deli Platters

THE BUCKINGHAMS
MERCY, MERCY, MERCY
YOU ARE GONE

4-44182

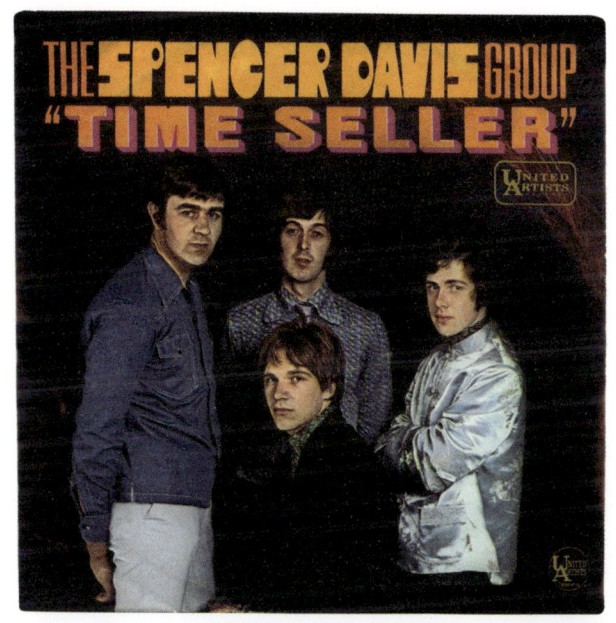

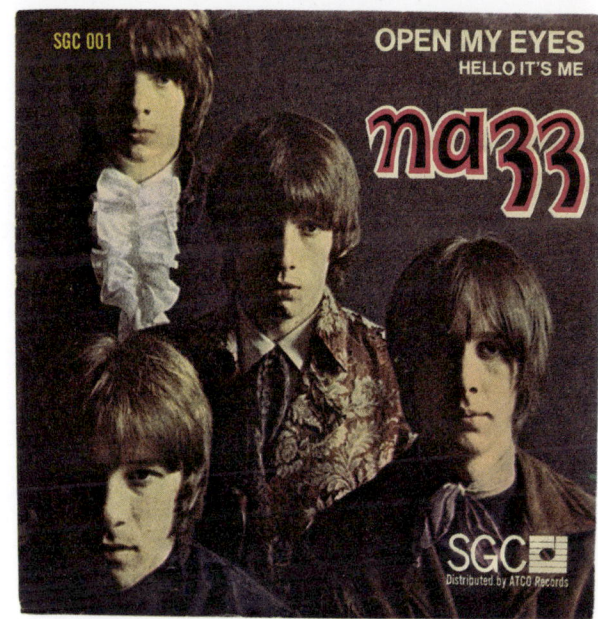

Don't Be Cruel • Hound Dog • My Baby Left Me
I Want You, I Need You, I Love You

EPA-940

The Real Elvis

Elvis Presley

RCA VICTOR
"NEW ORTHOPHONIC" HIGH FIDELITY RECORDING

© RCA Printed in U.S.A.

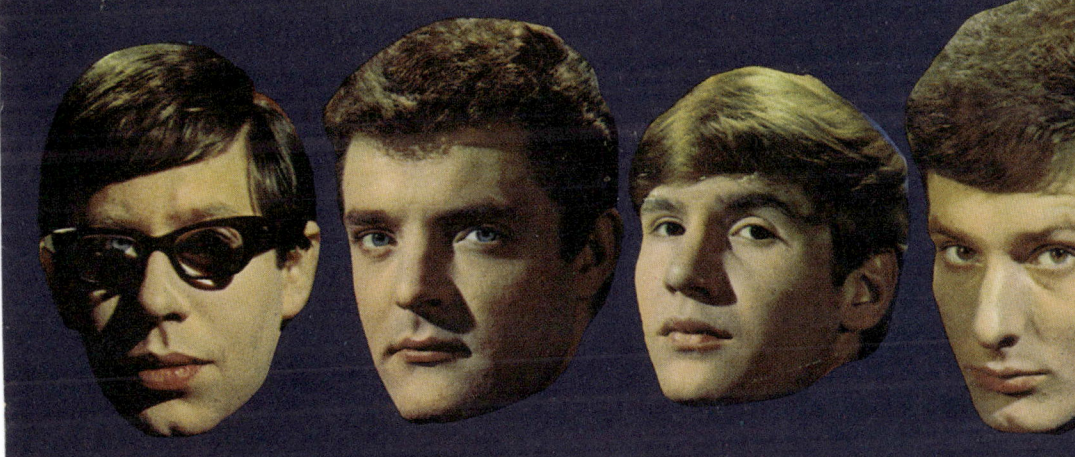

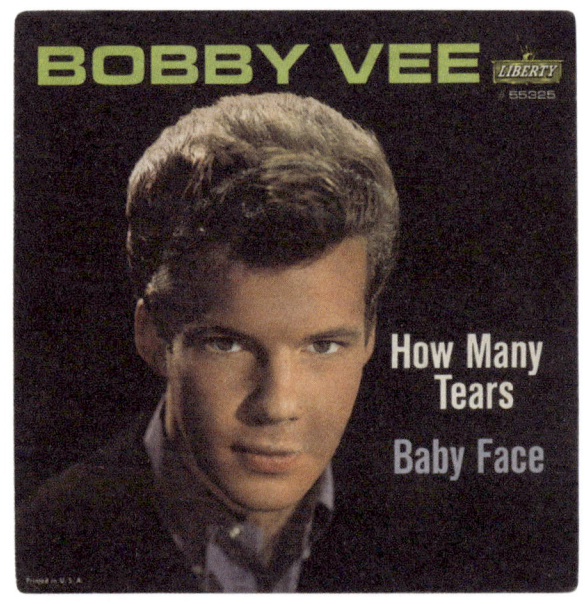

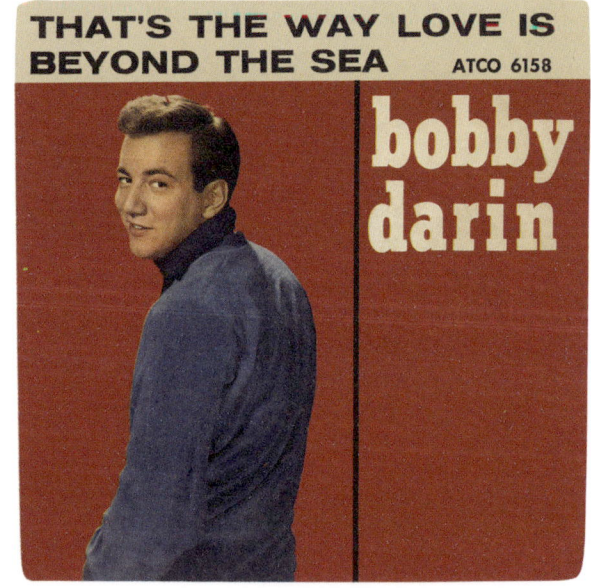

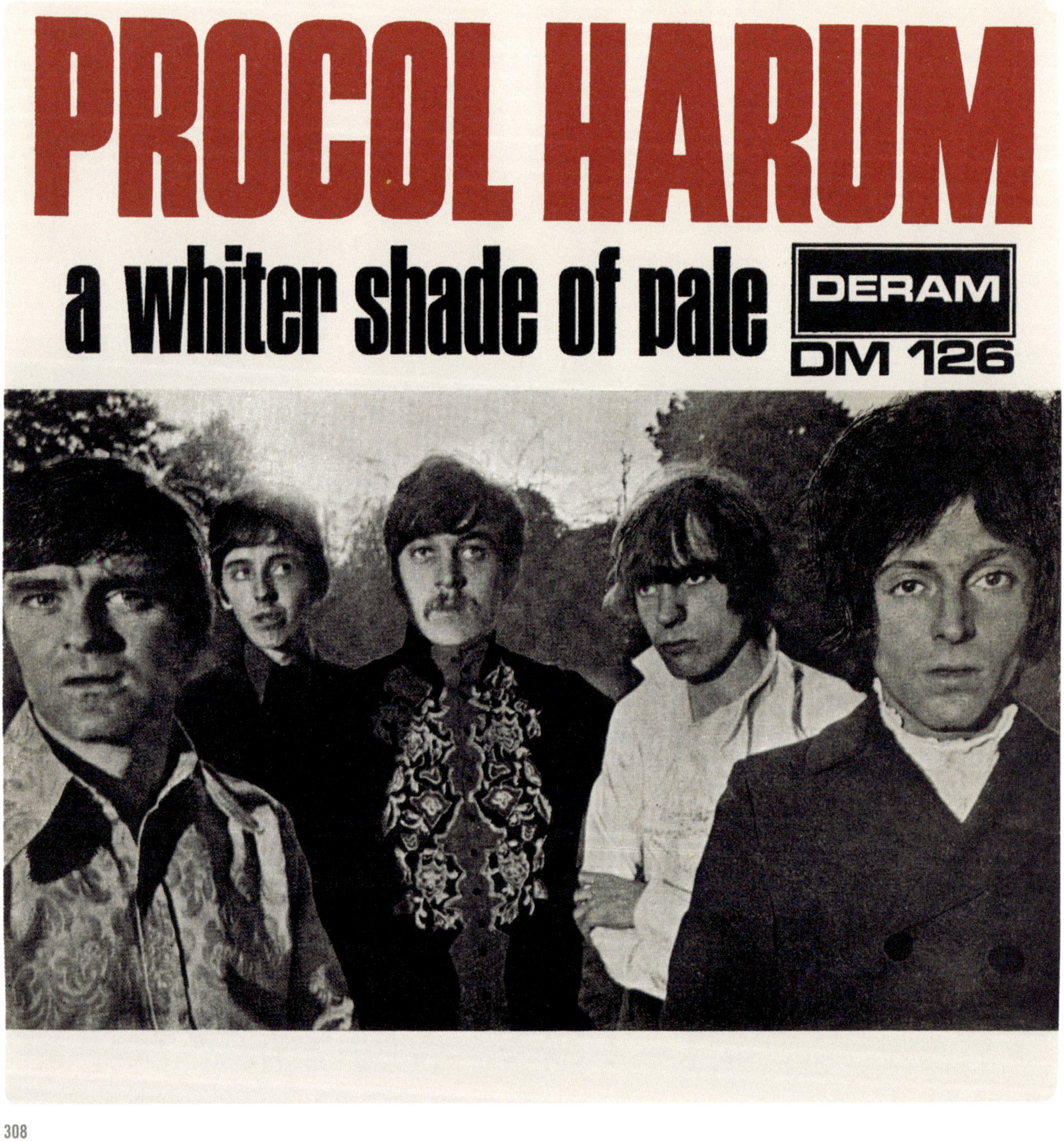

PROCOL HARUM
a whiter shade of pale

DM 126

ENGLAND'S NEWEST SINGING SENSATIONS

I'm Gonna Love You Too
Party Doll

R-4587

The Hullaballoos

RECORDED IN ENGLAND

BOB DYLAN
POSITIVELY 4th STREET
b/w
From a Buick 6

COLUMBIA

4-43389

ANDY GIBB

RS 872

"I Just Want To Be Your Everything"
B/W
"In The End"

© ℗ 1977 RSO RECORDS, INC.

Manufactured and Marketed by Polydor Incorporated. A Polygram Company.
810 Seventh Avenue, New York, NY 10019 · Distributed by Phonodisc Incorporated · Printed in U.S.A.

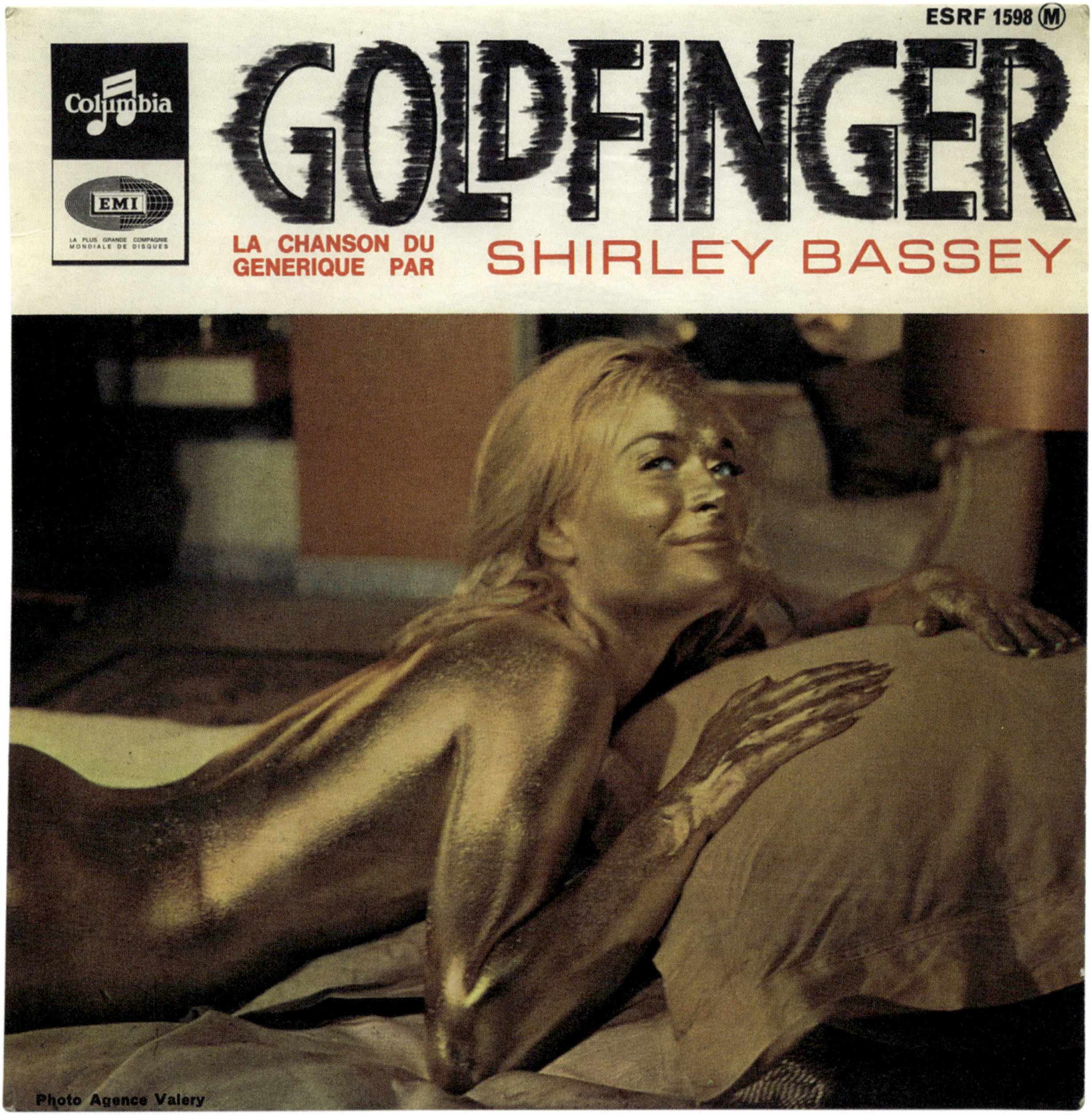

MUDHONEY

You Got It (Keep It Outta My Face)
b/w
Burn It Clean

SP33

FIFTEEN BUCKS
FOR
"FUCK HEAD"

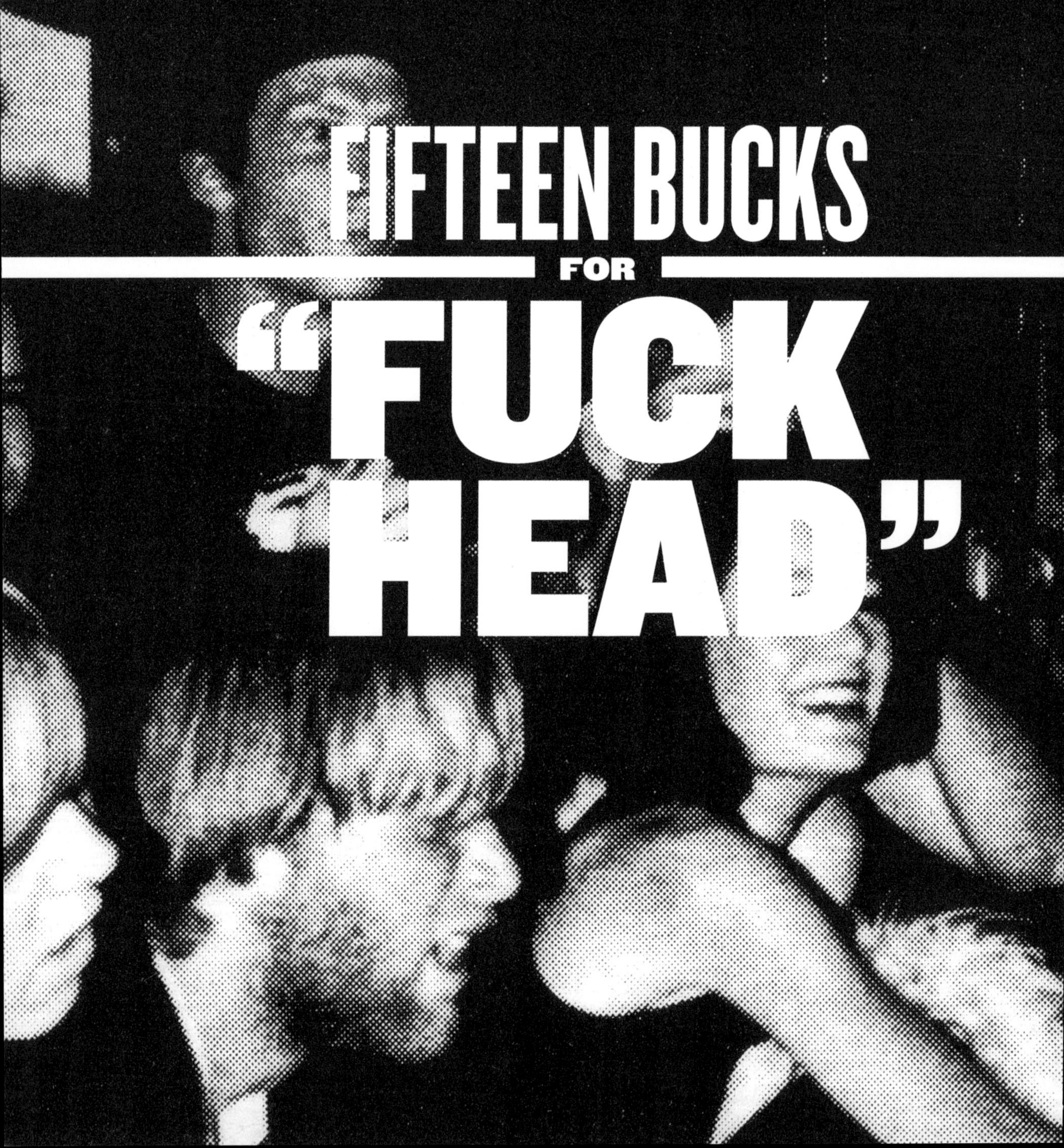

ERIC DAVIDSON

Fifteen bucks is a lot of dough to cough up for a thirty-second song called "Fuckhead." Or so say life's perpetual naysayers, like ex-girlfriends and mothers of the world. Hey, I'm not pointing fingers here—they can spend their fifteen dollars on lip gloss and blush. But when I walked into a record store one day in 1996 and found the Dwarves' "She's Dead"/"Fuckhead" 7-inch on Sub Pop—with that price tag sticking its tongue out at me—more conflicting excitement and shame flushed through me than any amount of face paint has ever inspired.

Up to that moment, I would've characterized myself as a record collector. A cheap two-dollar rockabilly comp stolen from a Woolworth's flipped the switch when I was fourteen. Years of scouring regional mom-and-pop music shops and biannual camp-outs at record conventions inside the United Auto Workers hall in Parma, Ohio, left me with a formidable wall of sound in my bedroom. (UAW halls, and the similarly paint-chipping chapels of the industrial age, Veterans of Foreign Wars halls, were often utilized throughout the rustbelt as metaphorically perfect dwellings for record conventions, themselves a graying old drinking buddy.) Then, in college, fate landed me in a dorm suite with a cat who could slay the guitar like he was swingin' a Pabst, and ten years later—fourteen years after that Woolworth's swipe—I was on tour as a singer with a Columbus, Ohio, punk band, New Bomb Turks, and found myself killing time in a record store.

Next to getting to travel with pals, play for fans, and flirt with the occasional daddy-issue dames, hitting up record stores was the best thing about touring. What other job allows you to travel from Mother Murphy's in Normal, Illinois, to Amoeba Music in L.A., then back home to Used Kids Records in Columbus, while spending entire afternoons gunking up your fingertips and lungs with dollar-bin dust? I've often wondered about record collectors who sat at home licking mail orders, or worse, trolling the superhighway Interweb for records when at least half the fun was yanking a decade-old holy grail out of a "10 for $5" box on the floor of some strip mall shop in a North Dakota suburb, while the old guy at the counter sighs in your general direction. This might've been the first clue that I wasn't a "real" record collector; I liked getting out of the house far too much for that.

As a member of a punk band, you spend more than you make, so shelling out most of my money on music may not have been the wisest move. And don't think this lapsed Catholic didn't shudder with guilt (withering, withering—gone!) when standing there in line at the counter debating. In one hand I held what would be my fourth copy of the first Velvet

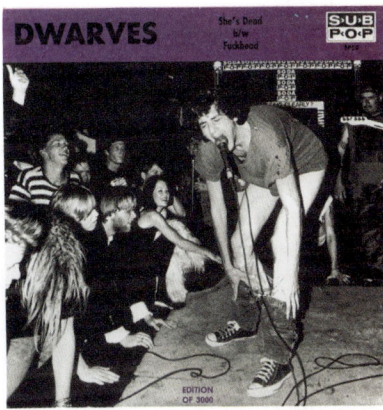

Underground record (hey, it's the one without the airbrush on the back cover!) and in the other, the Electric Eels' "Agitated," realizing that if I buy both, it'll put my total over $90, and I'll be lucky to clear $40 at that night's gig. "Um, do you take credit cards?"

The thing is, the first Velvet Underground album, an original edition of *Exile on Main St.*, or the Electric Eels' "Agitated" single are not only pinnacles of twentieth-century art, but unassailable collector's gold, hence easy to justify as the cashier rings them up. Surely someday I could trade this gem at five times as much to some Internet dork who wasn't lucky enough to be spending a sunny Saturday afternoon sitting on the grimy floor of a North Dakota record store.

But other records take far more self-goading. Which brings us to "Fuckhead." At the time, as an unrepentant Dwarves fanatic, my hands reached for that single like flies to an exquisitely beer-fed, Aussie bovine's dung heap. Ah, the Dwarves. Someday, in a bright and gleaming future, when AIDS has been cured, men have been rendered genetically impotent for lack of sperm demand (thanks to cryogenics and cloning), and all humans are a vague shade of light orange, there shall be true, liberating, morally untethered sex in the streets—and the Dwarves will be the soundtrack, blasted forth from the speakers of the government's roaming "Fluid Patrol" helio-scooters.

But in 1996, the Dwarves had gone through some profound demonic mutation from a late '80s neo-garage act to architects of the greatest rock 'n' roll record of all time, *Blood Guts & Pussy* (Sub Pop Records, 1990). On this record, a searing slice-n-dice of all fevered three-and-a-half-chord riffs flung around like crack babies spitting out Playdoh, if said infants were sexually deviant twenty-seven-year-old punks named stuff like Vadge Moore,

Salt Peter, and He Who Cannot Be Named; and whose habit of alley shtupping was surpassed in aggregate only by their intake of Pop Rocks, Coca-Cola, and cocaine. The LP ran eleven minutes, but it felt like five. And the "Fuckhead" 7-inch consisted of two songs left off of that masterpiece—I needed to have it.

I had been looking for this slab at a decent price for six years. At that moment, given the recent resurgence of vinyl singles, fifteen bucks seemed about right, especially given the fact that to this day, '90s Sub Pop singles, no matter who's on them, carry much collector weight. Still, even the price tag itself, handwritten by the store staff, implied that I was indeed a sucker for paying that much. All's fair in love and Dwarves.

Even by Dwarves' standards there was something really icky about the great cover art. Instead of the usual splashy colorful lettering or He Who Cannot Be Named's partially shaven, post-crab-nibbled crotch, this humble snapshot—singer Blag Jesus bending over, pants down (the closest to deference I've ever seen him offer to an audience), with mic in mouth when he knows any one of those slackers in the front row can gain momentary glory by yanking it out and besmirching his handsome visage—well, it was almost poignant.

Not to mention fucking hilarious. You don't even want to know what was on the back cover.

Suffice it to say, the songs on the single are swell, if understandably jettisoned from even an eleven-minute album. But in my eyes, the music on 45s is less than half the reason for nabbing them anyway, especially when lovingly swaddled in such shocking graphic design. Then, when I got home from that tour, I found out that both songs were on the CD of *Blood Guts & Pussy*, which came out a couple years after the vinyl, was—as always—a few more bucks than the record, and was, after all, a CD. So fuck that. Blag's just-out-of-sight jewels, the look on the burly bouncer's face, and the calm Helvetica of those song titles on the generic parody Sub Pop masthead—none of it could be found on that CD, which, of course, I bought later on anyway, probably for less than fifteen bucks.

Within the year after buying that single, I slowly realized that I make neither enough money, nor have patience with music any less butt-smashing than the Dwarves to spend fifteen dollars on any round bit of sound. Plus, being a freeloading rock critic, I get so many promos I rarely buy music of any sort. But the one thing I still spend some money on? Cool 45s, as long as they're about four bucks.

> **BUT IN MY EYES, THE MUSIC ON 45s IS LESS THAN HALF THE REASON FOR NABBING THEM ANYWAY, ESPECIALLY WHEN LOVINGLY SWADDLED IN SUCH SHOCKING GRAPHIC DESIGN.**

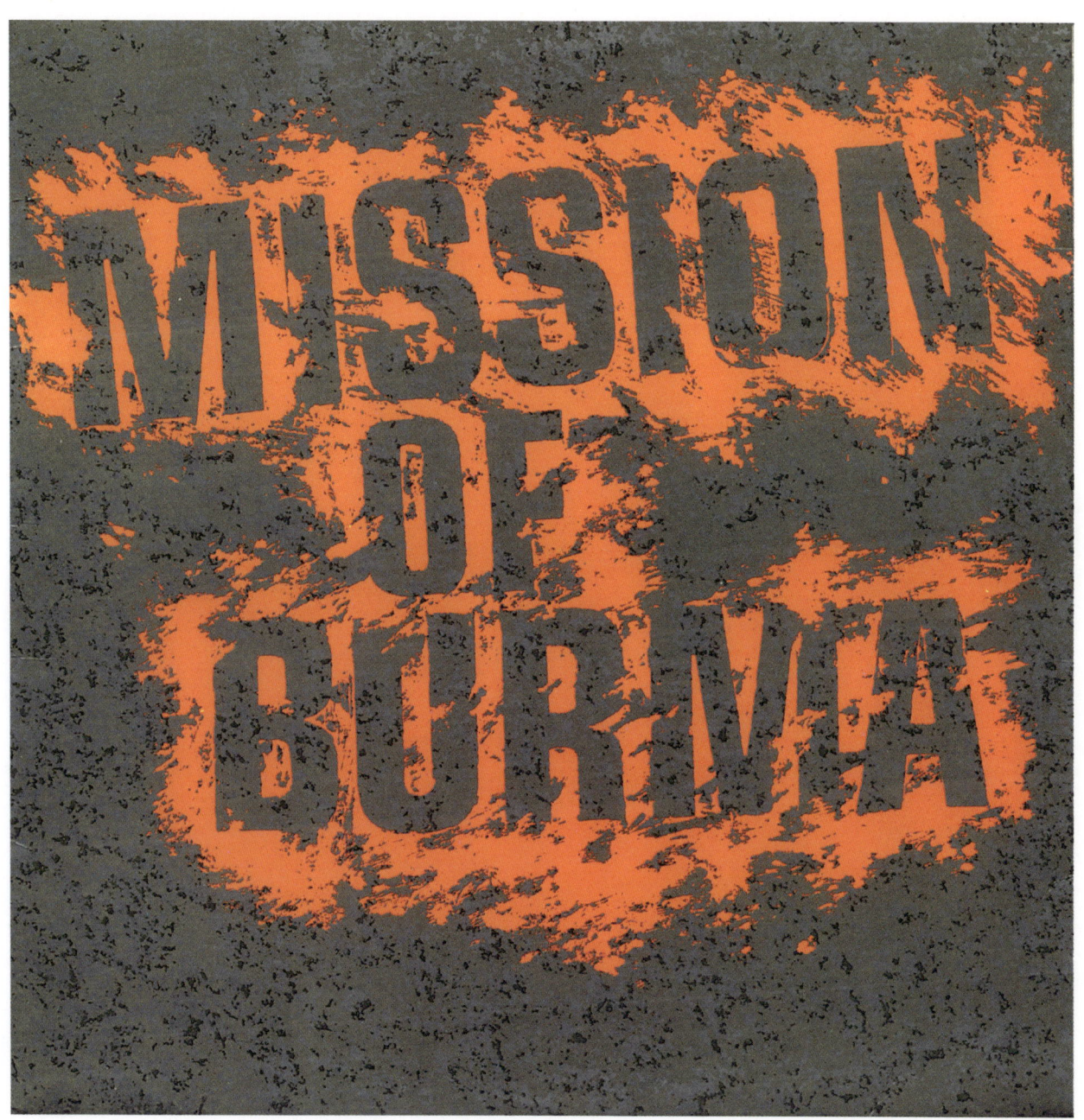

CRYING IN THE RAIN
b/w I'M NOT ANGRY
THE EVERLY BROTHERS

WARNER BROS.
HIGH FIDELITY
5250

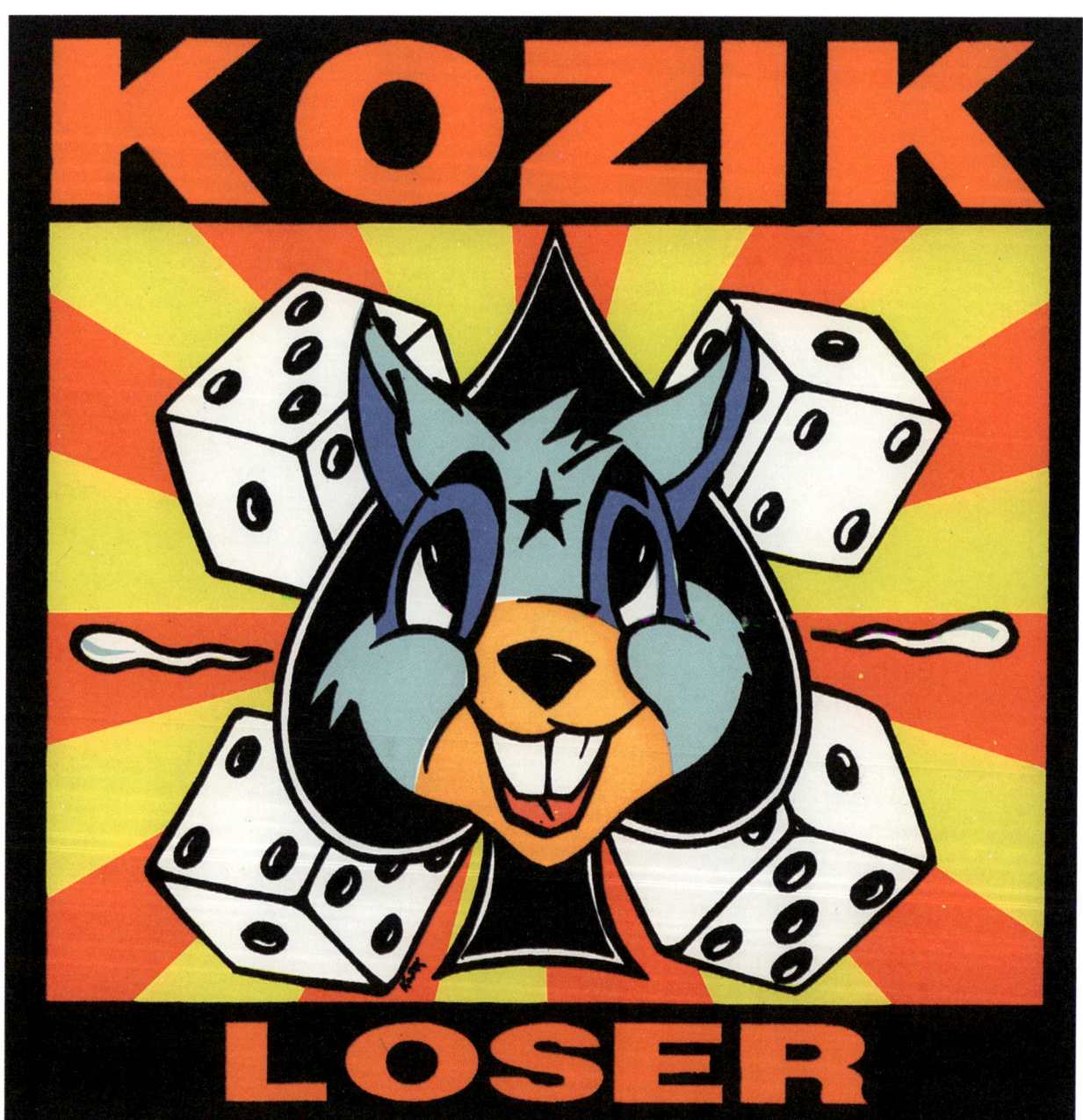

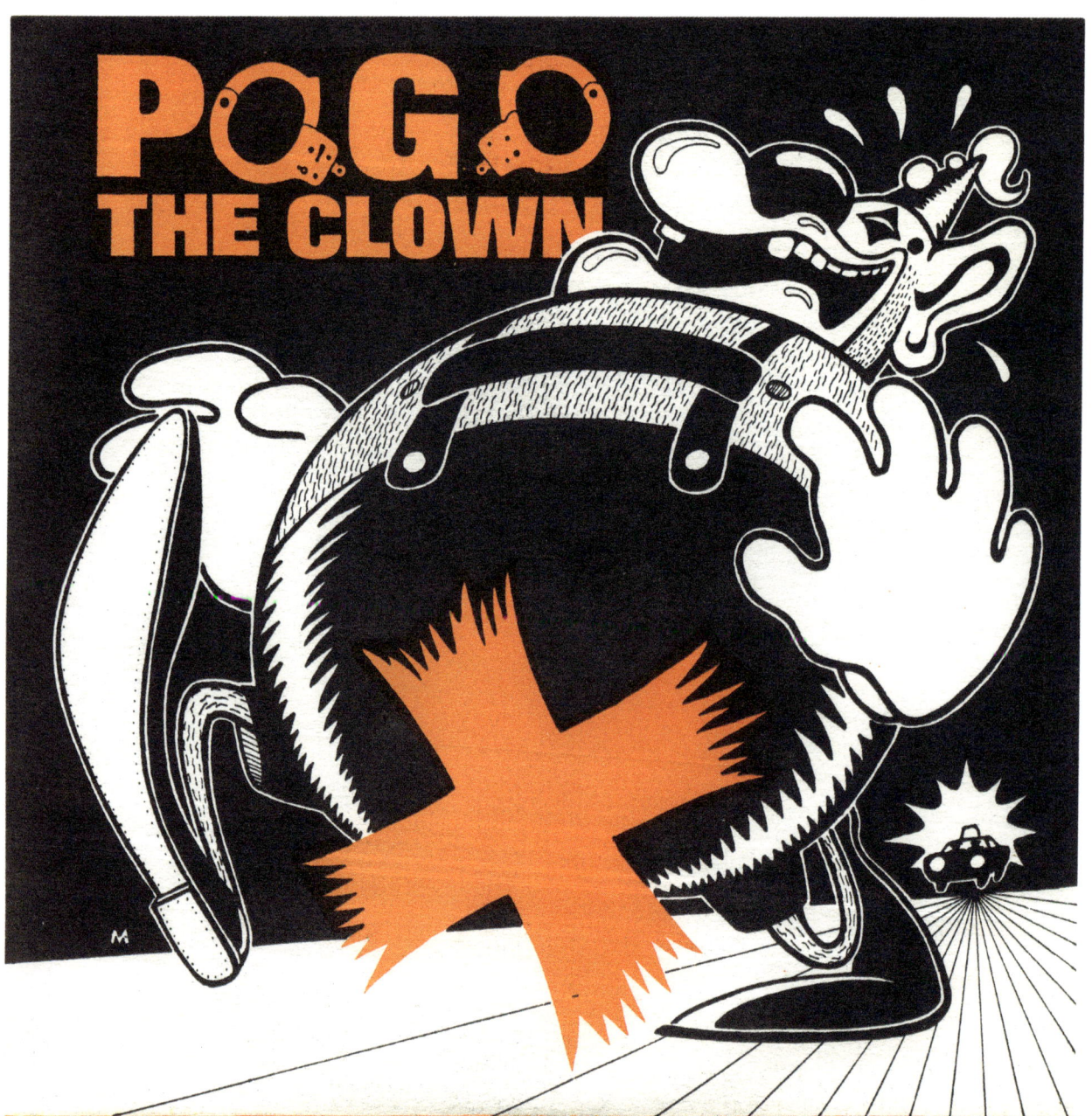

THE BEACH BOYS
HELP ME, RHONDA / KISS ME, BABY

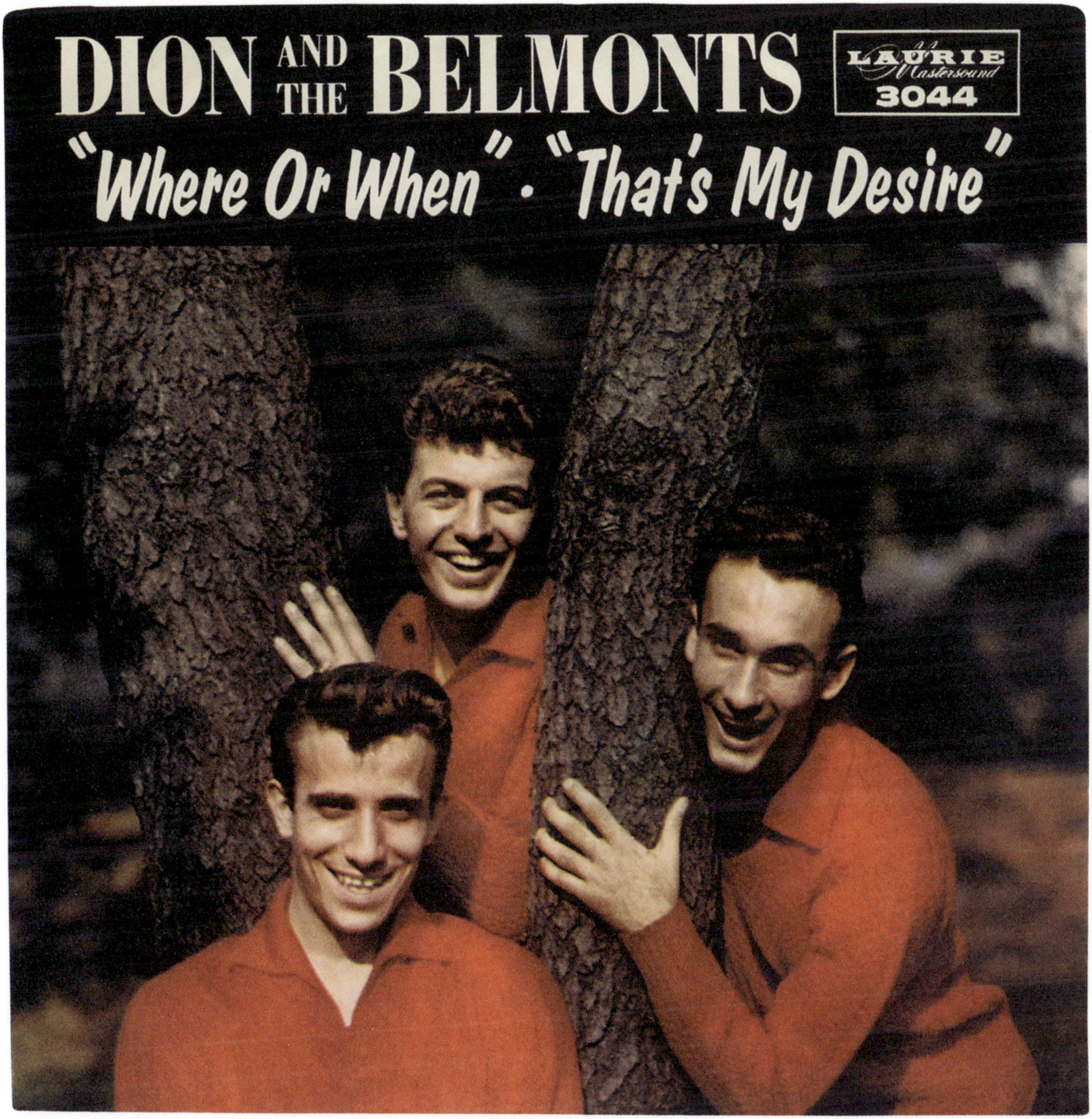

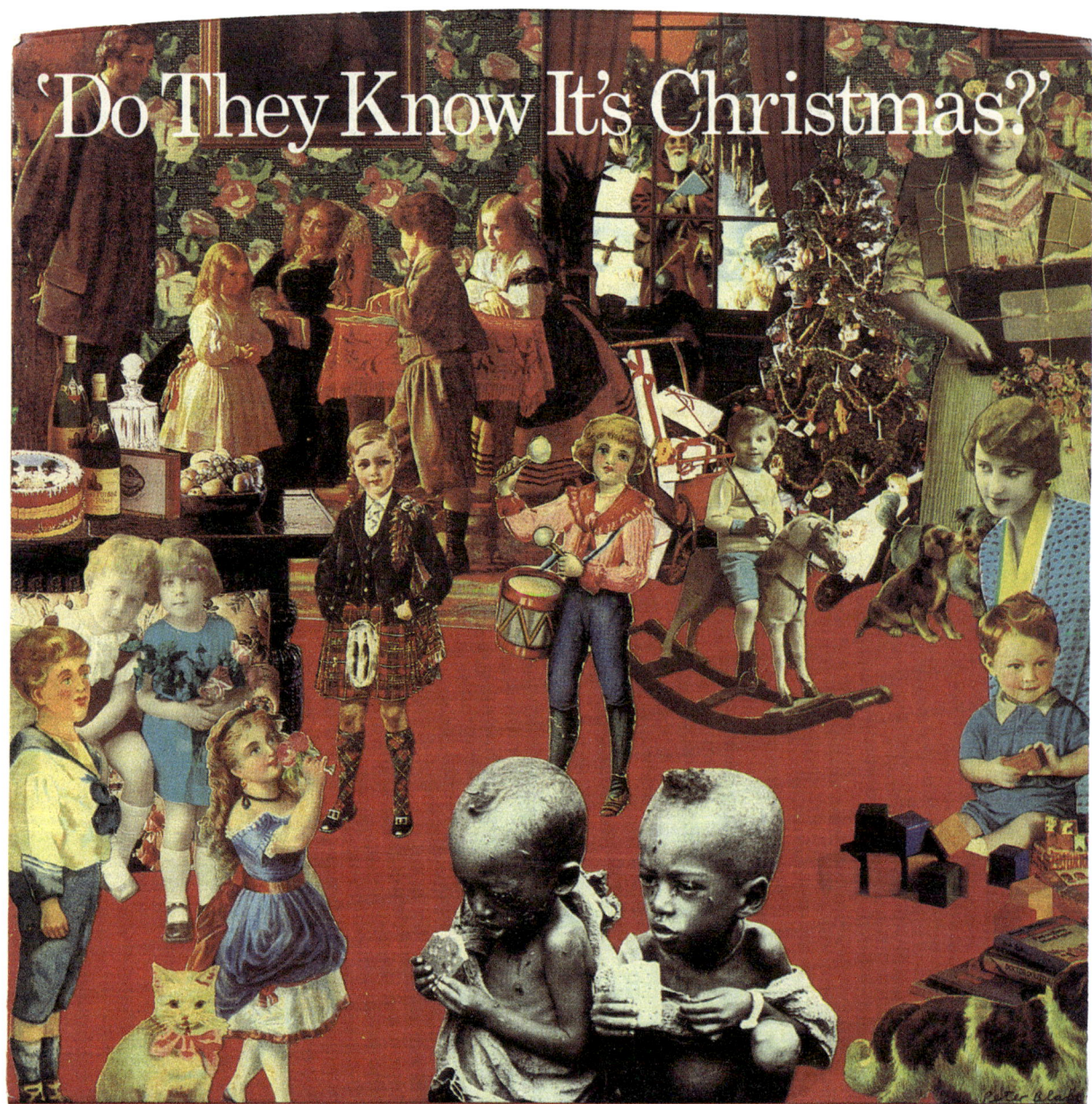

SUPERCHUNK

"the Majestic"

1999 Friends of Live Holiday Gift Limited Edition
1800 copies

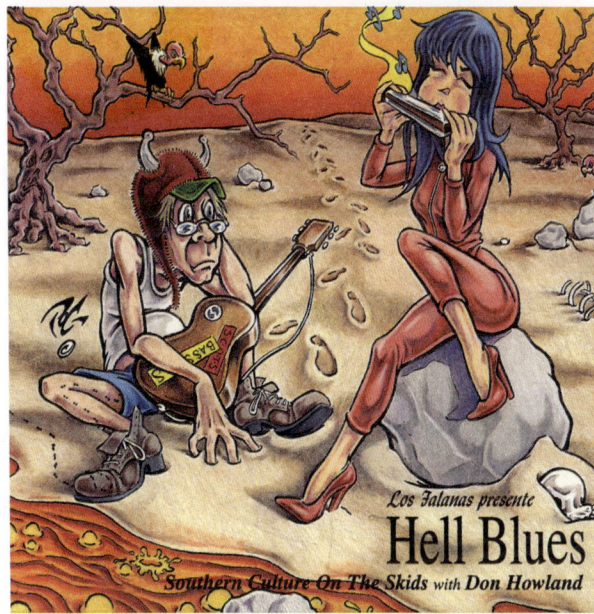

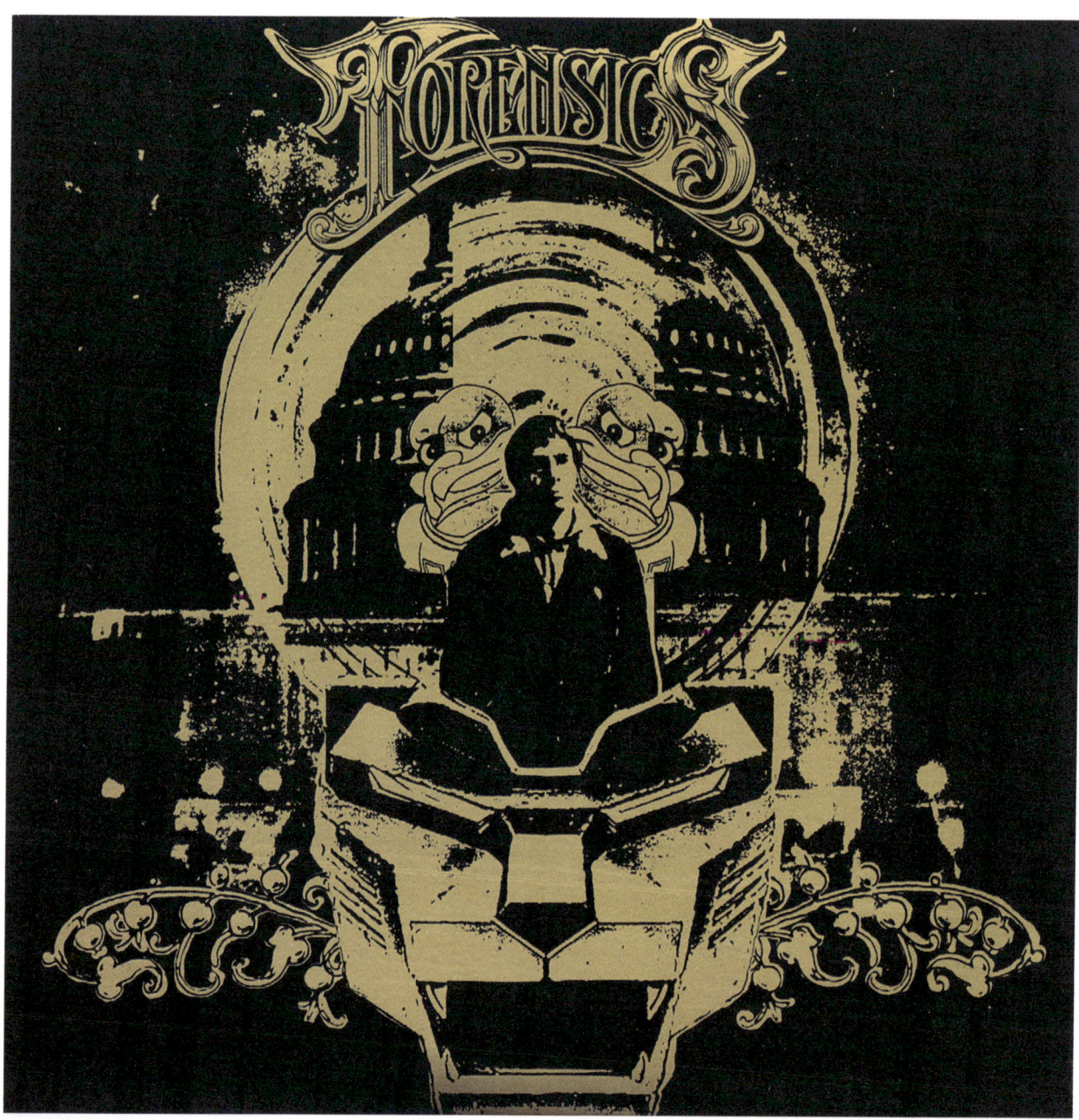

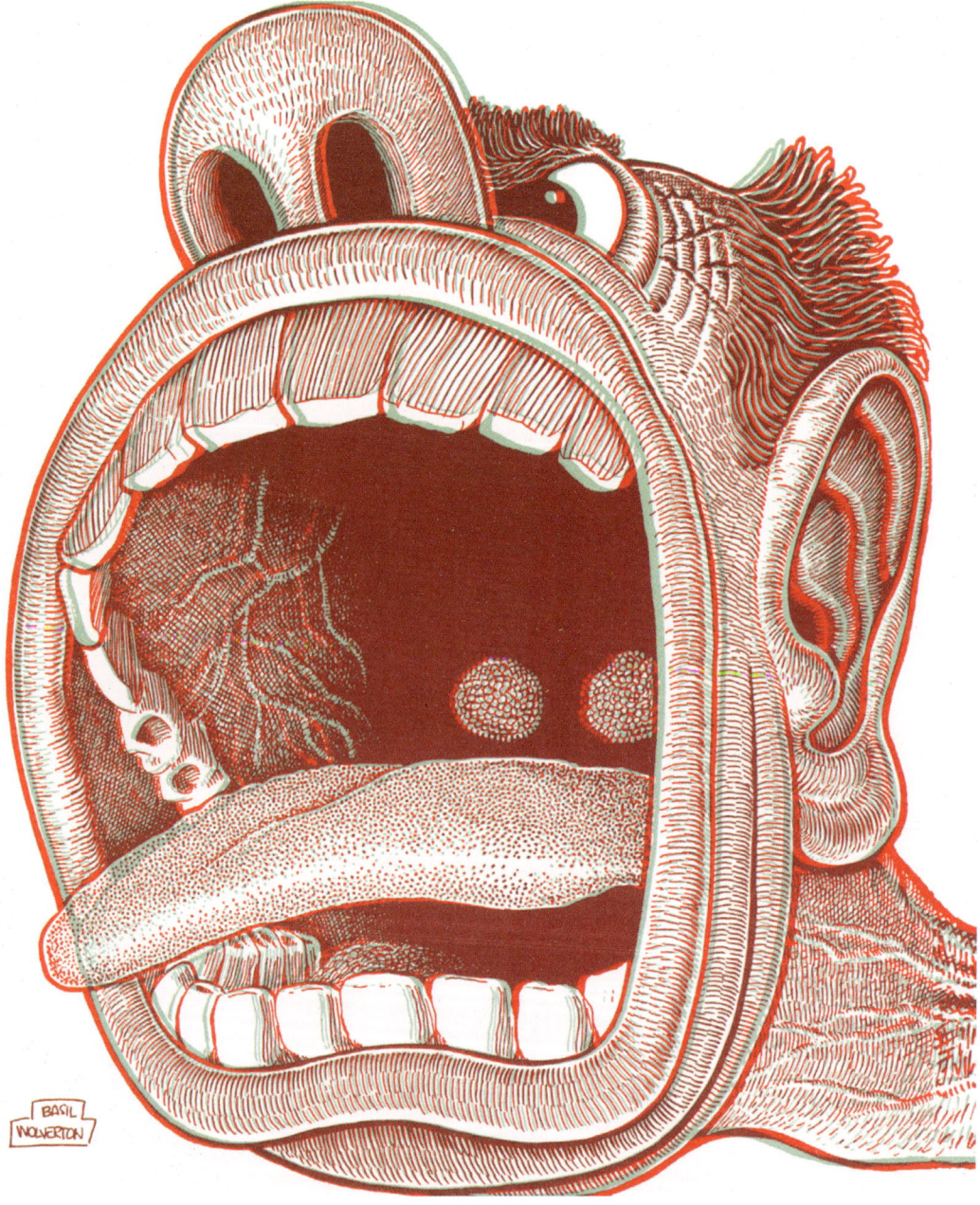

Rob Grigg on the drums.   We like to receive letters so it would be cool if you wrote to us at
e will try to write back.   In the USA we are managed by James McGarry who can be reached
THOSE WHO HAVE MADE US WELCOME IN THE PAST, AND WHO
ELCOME IN THE FUTURE.   IP041

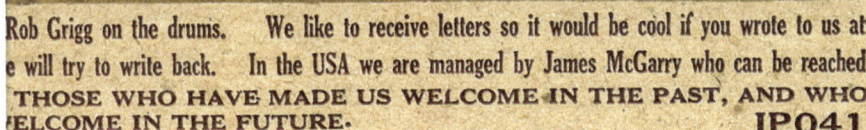

ON LETTERPRESS AND RECORD SLEEVES

BRUCE LICHER

It was early 1982 and I was looking for an artful and unique way to create a cover for an album I was recording with my group, Savage Republic. Fresh out of art school at UCLA, I wanted to make a record as if it were a limited edition piece of art. I happened upon a weekend class in letterpress printing at the Women's Graphic Center (WGC) in downtown Los Angeles and was immediately intrigued by the clanky, hand-fed machines. I was fascinated by the individual cast-metal letters—meticulously picked out of a drawer—and set them by hand, upside-down and backward. Designing for letterpress involved building a layout with numerous elements; hand-set metal type and ornaments, wood-mounted photo-engraving plates, carved linoleum blocks, hunks of metal or wood, and any other substance that was "type-high" could all be combined on press and created fresh and unusual results. The raised printing surfaces left an indentation on the printed piece, creating a textured, tactile object. It was as if one could feel the abrupt physical impact of metal onto paper, thereby revealing the power of the process. I discovered that almost any type of paper stock could be hand-fed into the press, from thin tissue paper to heavy chipboard card stock. I quickly began to visualize the potential to create a wide range of unique letterpress packaging and promotional materials for our music.

After learning the basics of letterpress by designing and printing a postcard advertising our forthcoming album, I set to work on a run of LP jackets using the WGC's large Vandercook cylinder press. I began by manually constructing blocks of type and other bits of imagery made from linoleum cuts and photo-engraved printing plates and then assembled them as you would a puzzle. Working intuitively, I locked the different pieces into the press with various archaic tools of the trade and figured out how the finished piece should look. The physicality of the process made me feel as if I were participating in an ancient, almost ritualistic craft. As I watched the slow, methodical operation of the press, hand-fed each sheet of paper, stopped to add ink when the printed image started to thin and fade, and set finished prints on the drying racks, I almost felt as if I was a part of the machine itself. Every printed piece that came off the press was subtly different—each one a hand-made yet mass-produced creation. Printed one color at a time, that first three-color run of 1,000 album jackets looked like nothing else you could find in the

record store bins at that time. Even now, more than twenty-five years later, the first edition of Savage Republic's debut album exudes an otherworldly essence.

By early 1983, Savage Republic had recorded another two songs and was prepared to release a 7-inch single. For the front cover I chose a photo of our flag flying in the wind, which I recreated on press using high-contrast, photo-engraved printing plates and a carved linoleum block surrounded by hand-set metal borders. The back cover layout consisted of blocks of hand-set type, plus several small graphic elements. For the final touches we added a print from the inked hand of our vocalist and a perforated commemorative stamp I'd created for the Republic. The single sold swiftly, and before long, a second pressing was needed. I had spent many days printing the first 1,000 sleeves and was not thrilled at the thought of doing the same thing all over again. Wanting to try something new, I discovered that I was able to move things around easily for this new run—or even reset the type if I decided I liked another font better than the ones I'd used the first time. I found that if I spent time blending inks, there was an almost infinite palette of ink colors available to me. The subtle redesign of the cover kept things interesting for me as artist and pressman, and I subsequently realized that the varying designs would make things more exciting for the record collectors of the future as well. I quickly embraced the idea of making each pressing unique. Since that single, every new edition or pressing of the band's recordings has been redesigned in one way or another. The fifth edition of the first Savage Republic album even had one entire run sent through the press upside down, so that some design elements that were meant to print on the front were printed on the back, and vice versa.

Today most letterpress-printed work is designed on a computer, with the final layouts etched onto photo-engraved metal or polymer printing plates—eliminating the element of hand-set type. This merging of old and new technologies provides an interesting contrast to the slick, Photoshopped artwork that is so prevalent in the music industry today but is still missing something. While the traditional result of the press may appear crude when compared to computer-generated graphic design, the work created by hand conveys a palpable intensity inherent to the letterpress process. Designing and printing on the press fosters a slower, more organic thought process, which requires the designer to be completely focused in the moment, while dealing with the challenges and limitations of the historic practice. Working with hand-set type and other hand-carved elements inherent to the "old-school" letterpress process is not only a more inspiring artistic experience for me as the designer, but results in a more authentic and emotional sleeve—a fitting home for the music within.

DESIGNING AND PRINTING ON THE PRESS...REQUIRES THE DESIGNER TO BE COMPLETELY FOCUSED IN THE MOMENT WHILE DEALING WITH THE CHALLENGES AND LIMITATIONS OF THE HISTORIC PRACTICE.

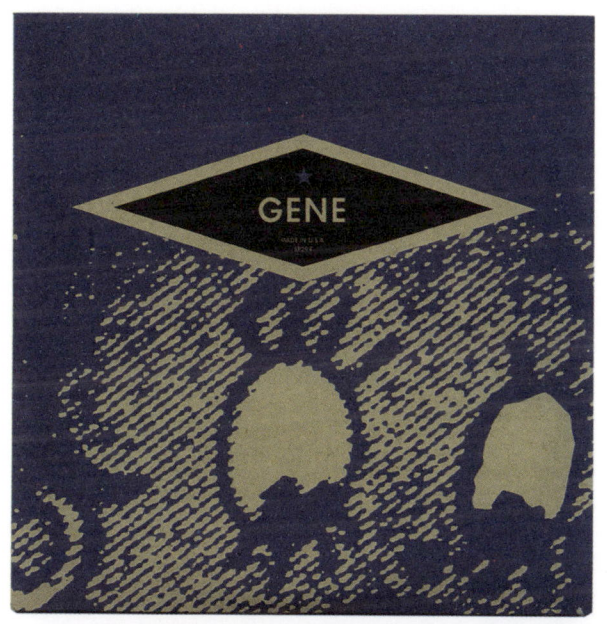

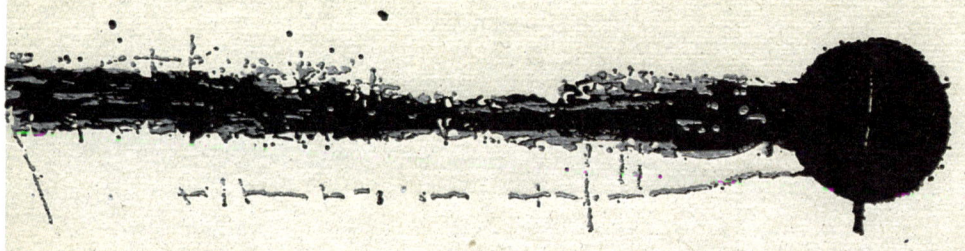

INDIAN BINGO
Big Rock

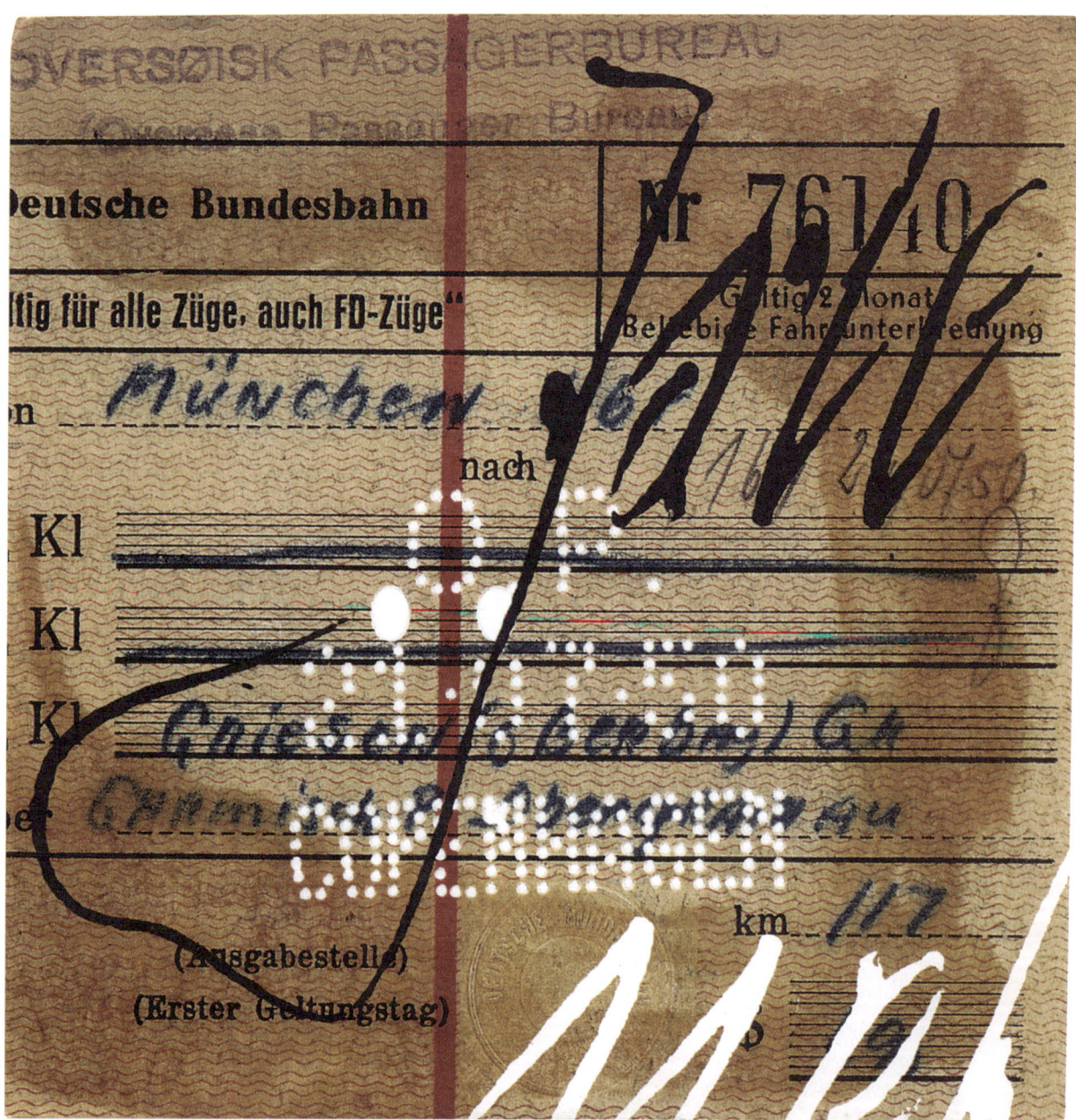

STYMIE

🛒 **Other**

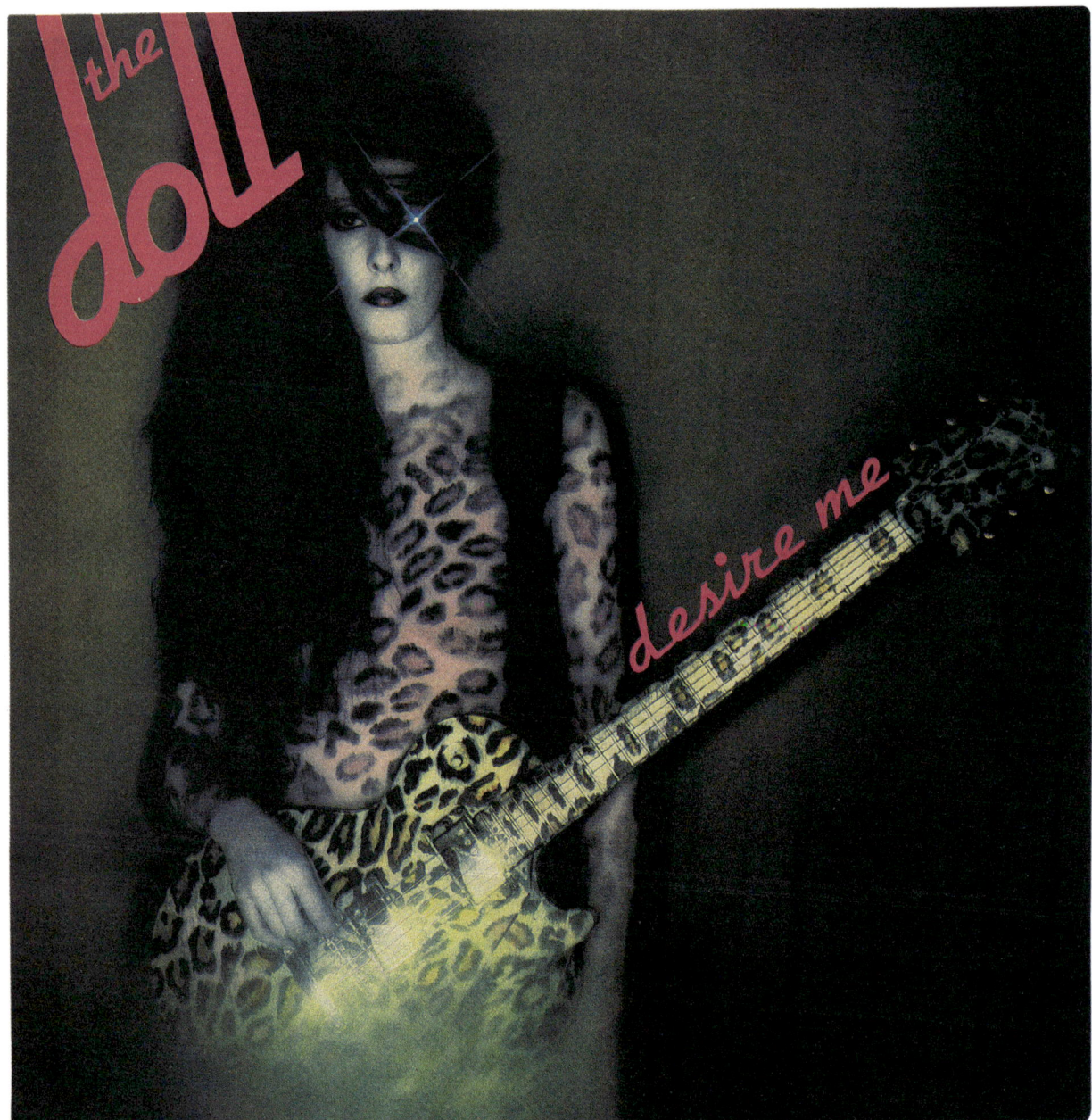

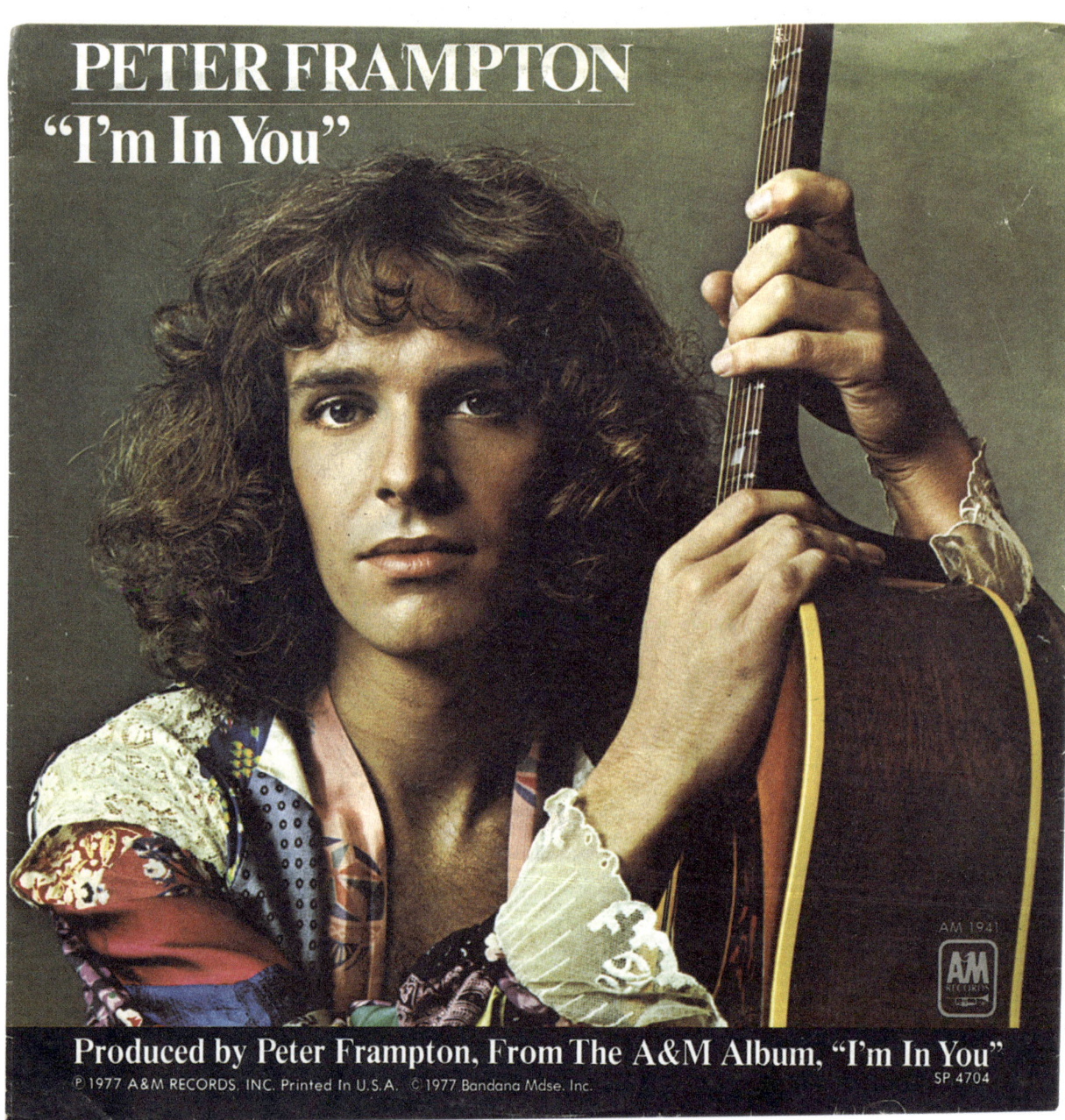

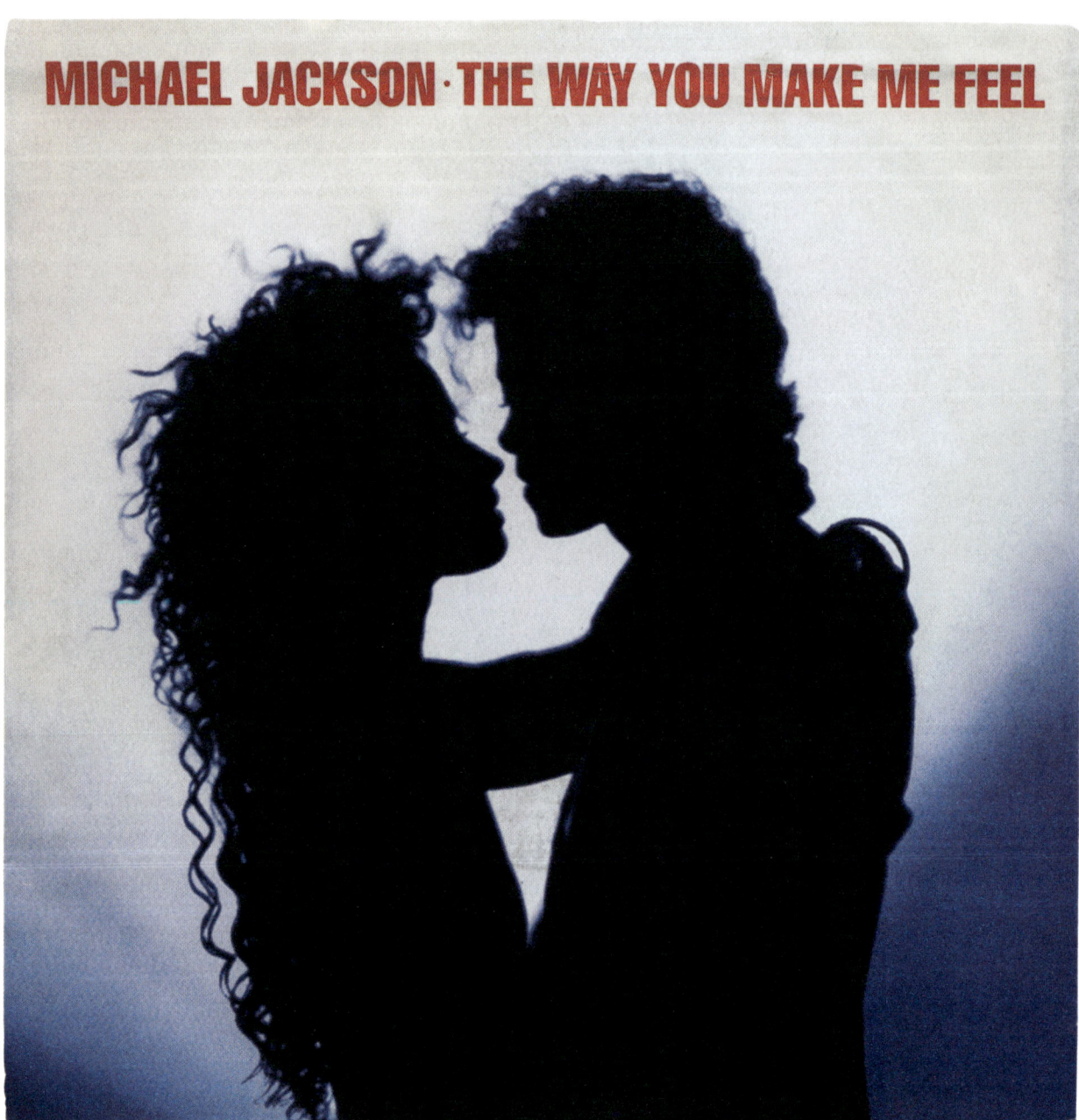

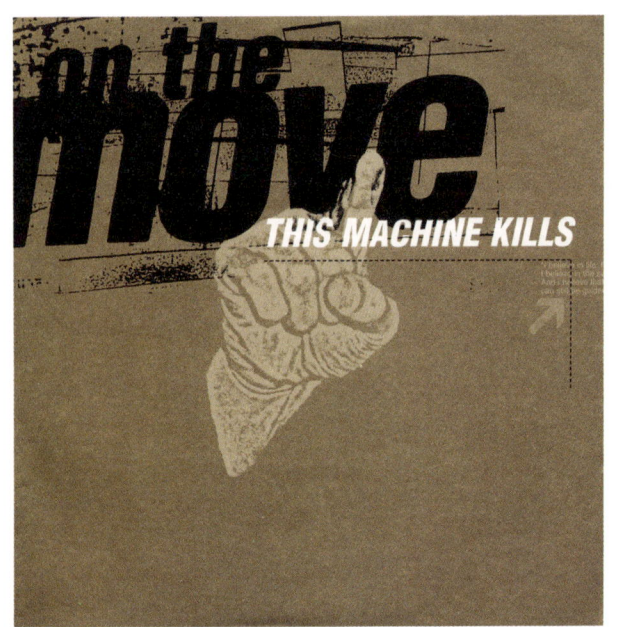
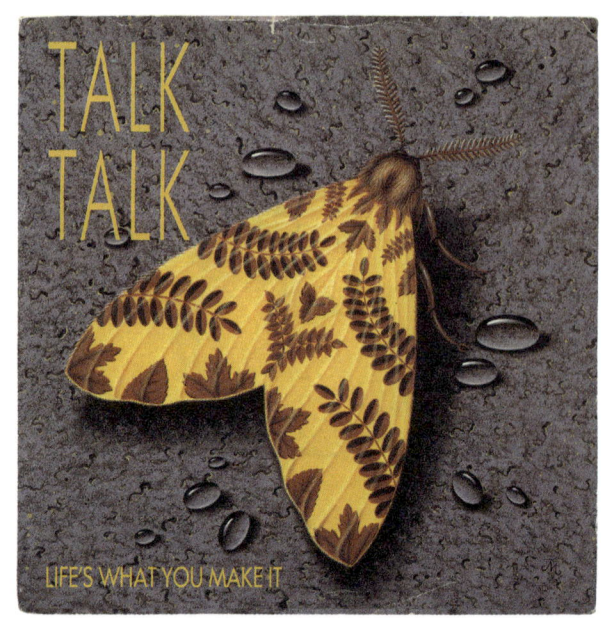

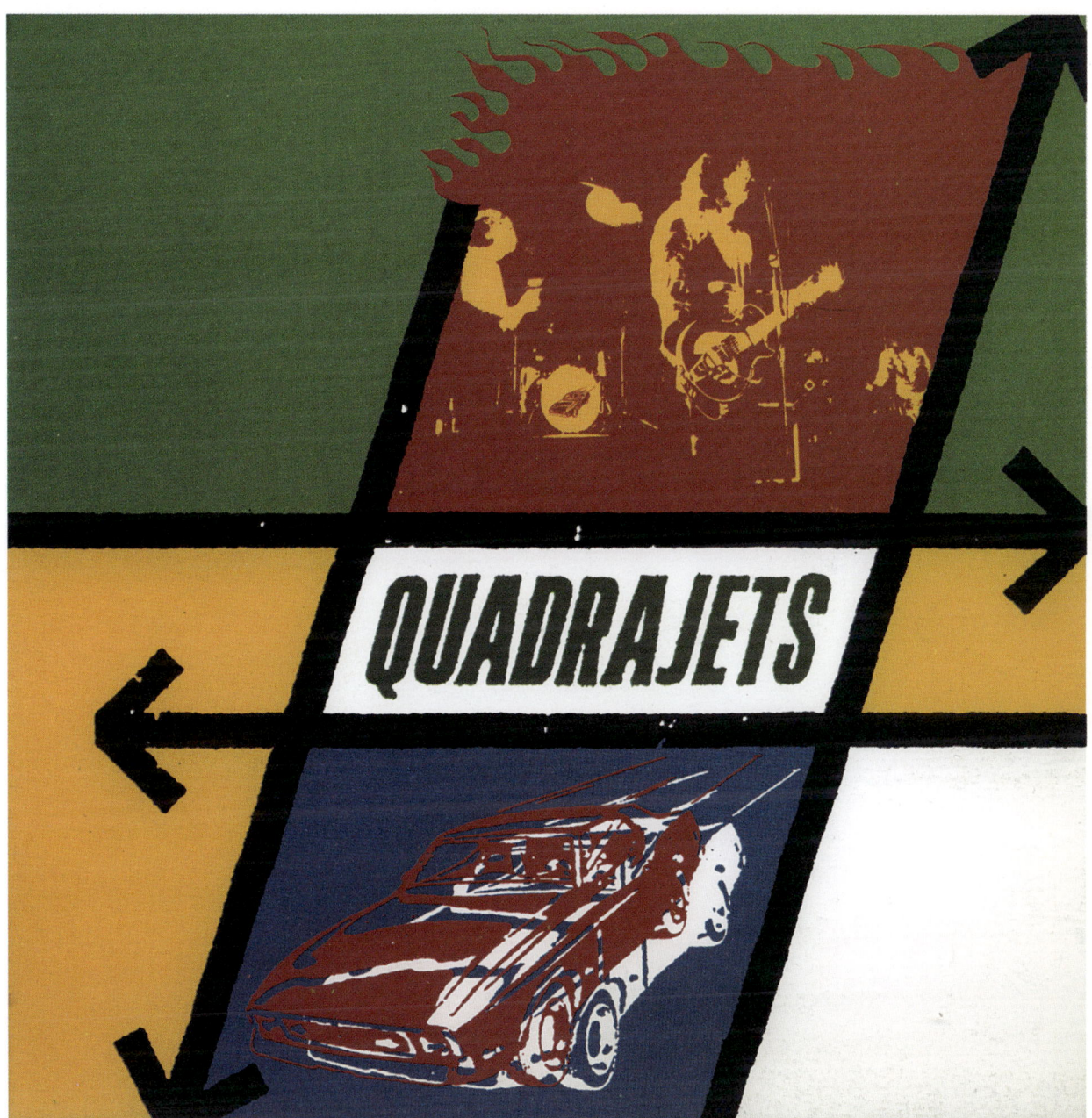

steel wool

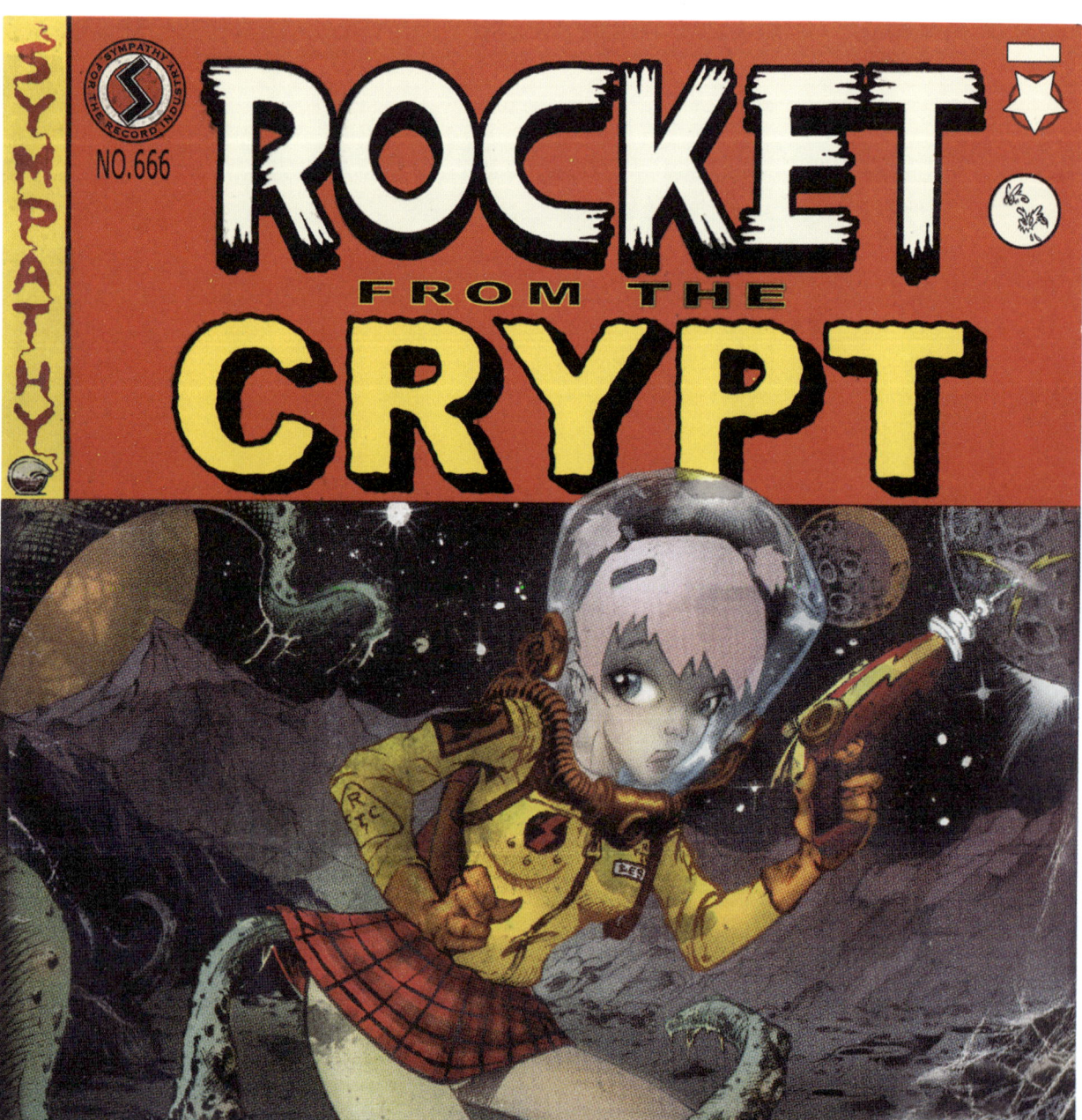

DIE ELECTRIC EELS

CYCLOTRON
FAUVIST MUSIK 2:04
BEI JOHN MORTON

TISCH

AGITATED
BEI DAVE E.
FAUVIST MUSIC 2:03

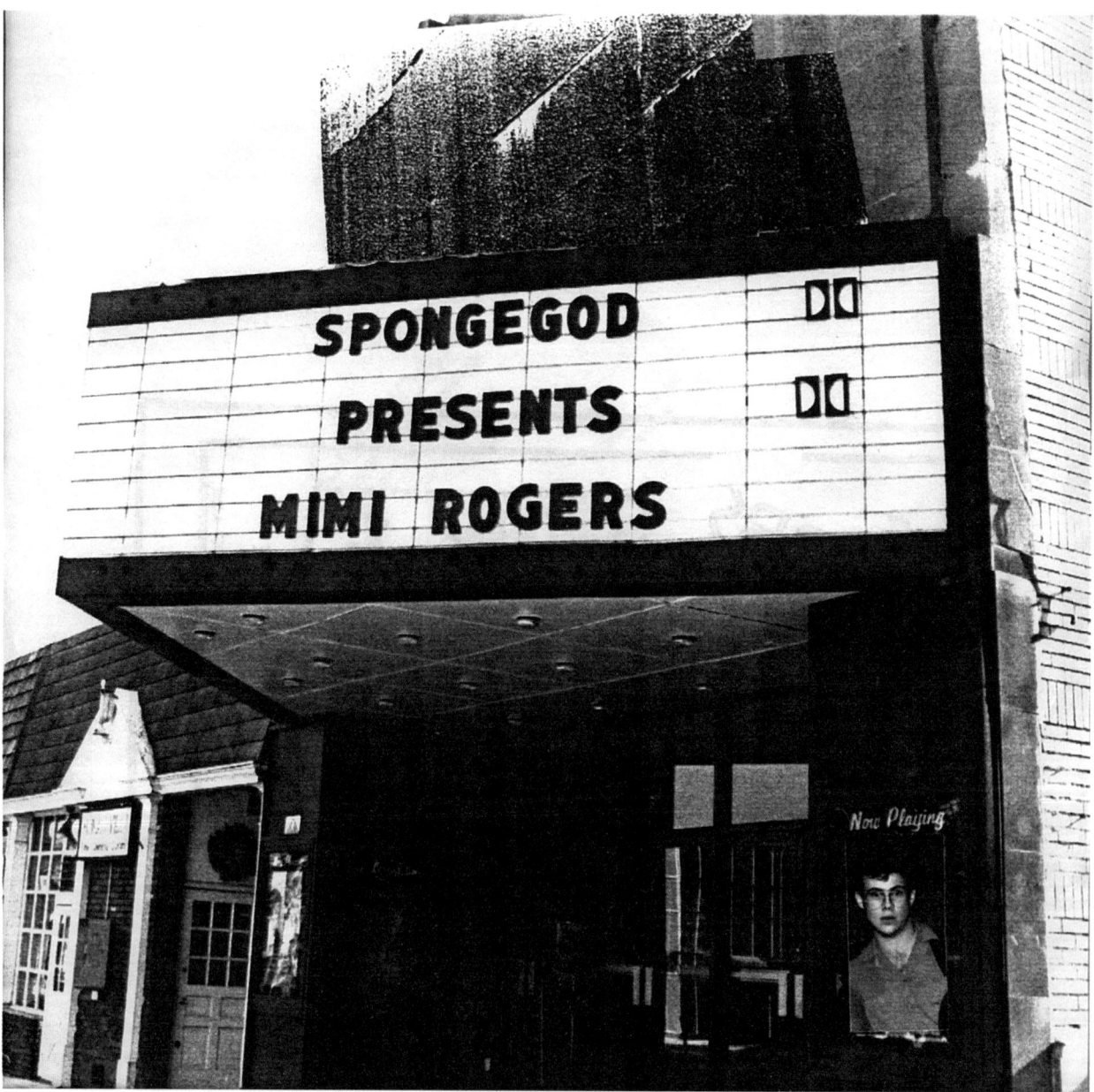

DISCOGRAPHY

1 **The Smithereens**
A Date With The Smithereens (No. 3)
RCA, 1994

2–3 **The Clash**
London Calling
CBS, 1979

4–5 **David Bowie**
Sorrow
RCA Victor, 1973

6 **Talking Heads**
Take Me To The River
Sire, 1978
Designers: Talking Heads and Spencer Drate

Joan Jett and the Blackhearts
Fake Friends
Blackheart Records, 1983
Photographer: Dieter Zill
Designers: Spencer Drate and Judith Salavetz

Talking Heads
Cities
Sire, 1980
Illustrator: Plastics
Designers: Talking Heads and Spencer Drate

9 **Lenny Kaye**
Child Bride
Mer, 1980
Photographer: Jody Caravaglia
Designer: Maude Gilman

10 **Bed Spring Motel with Roy Hall and His Jumping Cats**
Spring Street
Hi-Q, 1965

Dúo Dinámico
Bailando Twist
La Voz de Su Amor, 1962

12 **Talking Heads**
Once In A Lifetime
Sire, 1981

13 **XTC**
Love On A Farmboy's Wages
Virgin, 1983

14 **Calexico**
Drape
Bug Music, 1996

15 **Dave Davies**
Imaginations Real
RCA, 1980

16 **The Chills**
Rolling Moon
Flying Nun, 1982
Photographers and designers:
Terry Moore and Buzz

17 **Julie Driscoll, Brian Auger, and the Trinity**
This Wheel's On Fire
Marmalade, 1968

18 **Beat Happening**
Red Head Walking
Sub Pop, 1990

19 **Harry James and His Orchestra Featuring Helen Forrest**
I've Heard That Song Before
Columbia, 1942

20 **The Paley Brothers**
Ecstasy
Sire, 1977
Photographer: Eric Stephen Jacobs

21 **Surgery**
Feedback
Amphetamine Reptile, 1990

22 **Vetiver**
Hey Doll Baby
Gnomonsong, 2008
Illustrator: Nathaniel Russell

23 **The White Stripes**
Hello Operator
Sympathy for the Record Industry, 2000
Photographer: Ewolf
Designer: The Third Man

24 **Jet**
Cold Hard Bitch
Elektra, 2004

25 **Vertigo**
Driver #43
Amphetamine Reptile, 1993
Illustrator: Haze
Photographer: Corrigan

26 **The Beatles**
I Saw Her Standing There
Capitol, 1963

27 Clockwise from top left:
The Walker Brothers
Make It Easy On Yourself
Smash, 1965

The Four Seasons
Rag Doll
Philips, 1964

The Four Seasons
Ronnie
Philips, 1964

The Dave Clark Five
Everybody Knows (I Still Love You)
Epic, 1964

28 **Styrene-Money**
Jaguar Ride
Mustard, 1977

29 **The Adverts**
Gary Gilmore's Eyes
Anchor, 1977
Designer: Nicholas De Ville

30 **The Pogues**
Fairytale Of New York
Pogue Mahone, 1987

31 **Westside Lockers**
Fuchsia Rayon
Mr. Brown, 1980

32 **X**
Adult Books
Dangerhouse, 1978
Photographer and designer: Jules Bates

33 **The Cars**
Just What I Needed
Elektra/Asylum, 1978

34 **Pedro the Lion**
Sub Pop Singles Club
Sub Pop, 1999
Photographer: Josh Golden
Designer: Jesse Ledoux

35 **Monochrome**
Vara.45
Dim Mak, 2001
Photographer and designer: Helm Pfohl

36 **The Animals**
The House Of The Rising Sun
MGM, 1964

37 **The Rolling Stones**
Time Is On My Side
London, 1964

38 **The Beatles**
Help!
Capitol, 1965

39 Clockwise from top left:
Manfred Mann
Come Tomorrow
Ascot, 1965

Jan & Dean
Surf City
Liberty, 1963

The Turtles
Happy Together
White Whale, 1967

Jan & Dean
Drag City
Liberty, 1963

40 **The Cortinas**
Defiant Pose
Step Forward, 1977
Designer: TC&P

41 **XTC**
Making Plans For Nigel
Virgin, 1979
Illustrator: Steve Shotter
Designer: Cooke Key

42 **Grand Funk Railroad**
Take Me
Capitol, 1975

43 **Berlin**
Sex (I'm A...)
Geffen, 1982
Photographer: Ed Colver

44 **The Creatures**
Wild Things
Polydor, 1981
Photographer: Adrian Boot
Designer: Rob O'Connor

45 **David Bowie**
Diamond Dogs
RCA, 1983

46 **El Vez**
The Mexican Elvis
Sympathy for the Record Industry, 1991

47 **Elvis**
Rock-A-Hula Baby
RCA Victor, 1961

48 **The Everly Brothers**
Stick With Me Baby
Warner Brothers, 1961

49 **The Beach Boys**
Little Honda
Capitol, 1964

50 **Living Stereo**
Sounds In Space
RCA Victor, 1958

51 **The B-52's**
Rock Lobster
BMI, 1978
Photographer: Ann States

52 **The Rolling Stones**
Love Is Strong
Virgin, 1994
Illustrator: Christian Piper
Designer: Mark Norton

53 **The Fridges**
E.P.
Ink Ink, 1980

54 **13th Floor Elevators**
You're Gonna Miss Me
Radarscope, 1978
Makeup: Djakasta

55 **The Police**
De Do Do Do, De Da Da Da
A&M, 1980

56 **The Kinks**
David Watts
Pye, 1967

57 **Sly & The Family Stone**
Everyday People
Epic, 1968

58 **Talking Heads**
Burning Down The House
Sire, 1983

59 Clockwise from top left:
Multiple Artists
2 Legs Bad. 38 Legs Good
The Magic Bullet, 2003

Blood Brothers
Love Rhymes With Hideous Car Wreck
Dim Mak, 2003
Designer: Julian Grass

Mazarin
Memories Change in Patterns
Sub Pop, 2002

Saturday Looks Good to Me
Money In The Afterlife
Ernest Jenning, 2007
Illustrator: Sally Oviatt

60 **The Phantom Surfers**
Unknown Museum Stomp
Sympathy for the Record Industry, 1992
Illustrator: Coop

61 **Ramleh**
8 Ball Corner Pocket
Sympathy for the Record Industry, 1993
Illustrator: Pablo (The Frozen One)

62 **Multiple Artists**
Things That Are Heavy
New Rage, 1992

63 **The Lovin' Spoonful**
Six O'Clock
Kama Sutra, 1967

64 **Paul Anka**
Love Me Warm And Tender
RCA Victor, 1962

65 **The Deadbeats**
Kill The Hippies
Dangerhouse, 1978
Designer: David Williams

66 **The Art Attacks**
I Am A Dalek
Albatross, 1978

67 **Hammerhead**
Duh, The Big City
Amphetamine Reptile, 1994

68 **George Burns**
I Wish I Was Eighteen Again
Mercury, 1979

69 **Richard Lloyd**
Get Off Of My Cloud
Ice Water Music, 1981

70 **Frank Sinatra**
Songs For Young Lovers
Capitol, 1955
Photographer: Ken Veeder

71 **Nat King Cole**
Just One Of Those Things
Capitol, 1957

72 **The Sports**
So Obvious
Stiff, 1979

73 **The Beach Boys**
I Just Wasn't Made For These Times
Sub Pop, 1996

74 **Ron Haydock**
Sounds Like
Norton, 1996
Cover Art: Big Al

75 **Lulu**
Try To Understand
Decca, 1965

76 **The Left Banke**
Walk Away Renee
Bam Caruso, 1983
Designers: Cally and Phil at Waldo's Design

77 **Sex Pistols**
Pretty Vacant
Virgin, 1977

78 **Girls At Our Best**
Getting Nowhere Fast
Record Records, 1980

79 **Talking Heads**
Love → Building On Fire
Sire, 1977
Photographer: Jimmy DeSana

81 **Elvis Presley**
Teddy Bear
RCA Victor, 1957

82 **Elvis Presley**
Devil In Disguise
RCA Victor, 1963

Bob Dylan
Subterranean Homesick Blues
Columbia, 1965

84 **Madness**
Work Rest & Play
Stiff, 1980

85 **The B-52's**
Rock Lobster
Island, 1979

86 **Countdowns**
Ghetto Blaster
Scooch Pooch, 1996
Designer: Hank Trotter

87 **The Smithereens**
A Date With The Smithereens (No. 3)
RCA, 1994

88 **Ramones**
The Blitzkrieg Bop!!
Sire, 1976

89 **Young Fresh Fellows & Scruffy the Cat**
VS.
Cruddy, 1989
Illustrators and designers: Tad Hutchison and Kurt Bloch

90 **The Beatles**
Paperback Writer
Capitol, 1966

91 **Dead Boys**
Tell Me
Sire, 1978
Designer: Spencer Drate

92 **The Union Gap**
Young Girl
Columbia, 1968

93 **Paul Revere and the Raiders**
Hungry
Columbia, 1966

94 **The Avengers**
We Are The One
Dangerhouse, 1977

95 **The Shins**
New Slang
Sub Pop, 2001

96 **Tina Peel**
More Than Just Good Looks
Dacoit/Limp, 1978

97 **The Immortal Lee County Killers**
Let's Get Killed
Estrus, 2001
Designer: Art Chantry

98 **The Yardbirds**
Over, Under, Sideways, Down
Epic, 1965

99 **The Who**
Dogs
Polydor, 1968

100 **Three Dog Night**
Mama Told Me (Not To Come)
Dunhill, 1970

101 **Gary Lewis and the Playboys**
Everybody Loves A Clown
Liberty, 1965

102 **The Rolling Stones**
Undercover Of The Night
Rolling Stones, 1983
Cover art: Hubert Kretzschmar
Designer: Peter Corriston

103 Clockwise from top left:
Sham 69
You're A Better Man Than I
Polydor, 1979
Photographer: Adrian Boot
Designer: Jo Mirowski

The Clash
Tommy Gun
CBS, 1978

Darling
Voice On The Radio
Charisma, 1979
Designer: Rocking Russian

Helmet
Primitive
Amphetamine Reptile, 1993
Designer: Haze

104 **The Adverts**
Safety In Numbers
Anchor, 1977
Designer: Nicholas De Ville

105 **The Young Rascals**
People Got To Be Free
Atlantic, 1968

106 **Tours**
Language School
Tours, 1979

107 **Frankie Valli**
I Make A Fool Of Myself
Philips, 1967

108 **Bob Dylan**
Can You Please Crawl Out Your Window?
Columbia, 1965

109 **The Four Seasons**
Why Do Fools Fall In Love
Vee Jay, 1963
Photographer: Otto Fenn
Designer: Bob Crewe

110 **The Ronettes**
Born To Be Together
Philles, 1965

111 **The Supremes**
You Keep Me Hangin' On
Motown, 1966

112 **Connie Francis**
I'm Gonna' Be Warm This Winter
MGM, 1963

113 **Joni James**
Let There Be Love
MGM, 1956

114 **Blondie**
Atomic
Chrysalis, 1980

115 **The Rolling Stones**
Angie
Rolling Stones, 1973

116 **The Rolling Stones**
She's So Cold
Rolling Stones, 1980

117 **Moby**
That's When I Reach For My Revolver
Sub Pop, 1996

118 **Mudhoney and Jimmy Dale Gilmore**
Tonight I Think I'm Gonna Go Downtown
Sub Pop, 1994
Illustrator: Edwin Fotheringham
Designer: Jeff Kleinsmith

119 **Dee Rangers**
This Is Not The Modern World
Estrus, 1998
Designer: Art Chantry

120 **Los Marauders**
Live From Amamosa Womens Prison
Estrus, 1995
Designer: Hank Trotter

121 **Control Freak and Stymie**
S.O.U.S
New Rage/Cavity Search, 1995
Designer: Jeff Kleinsmith

122 **The Seeds**
Can't Seem To Make You Mine
GNP Crescendo Records, 1967

123 **Traffic**
Hole In My Shoe
United Artists, 1967

124 **The Beatles**
Yes It Is
Capitol, 1965

125 **The Rolling Stones**
The Last Time
London, 1965

126 **The Spotnicks**
Orange Blossom Special
President, 1962

127 **Supernova**
How Much More
Sympathy for the Record Industry, 1996

128 **The Rolling Stones**
Out Of Tears
Virgin, 1994

129 **U-Men**
Freezebomb
Amphetamine Reptile, 1988

130 **Chain Gang**
Son Of Sam
Kapitalist, 1977

131 **XTC**
Generals And Majors
Virgin, 1980
Designer: Jill Mumford

132 **The Hellacopters**
Slow Down Take A Look
Sub Pop, 1999
Photographer: Lance Hammond
Designer: Jeff Kleinsmith

133 **The Datsons (The High Dials)**
Thief In The Night
Ricochet Sound, 2001
Photographer: Meliza Ash
Designer: Dean Sterling

134 **The Rolling Stones**
Mother's Little Helper
London, 1966

135 **The Rolling Stones**
Let's Spend The Night Together
London, 1967

136 **The Rolling Stones**
Before They Make Me Run
Rolling Stones, 1978
Photographer: Annie Leibovitz

137 Clockwise from top left:
The Damned
Neat Neat Neat
Stiff, 1977

The Billy Syndrome
Secret
Slutfish Records, 1996
Photographer: André Grossmann
Art Director: Bill Ogilvie

Yardbirds
Over, Under, Sideways, Down
Edsel, 1966
Photographer and designer: Chris Dreja

The Fuckers
Block Party
Sup Pop, 1992
Photographer: Drew Donley

138 **Ann-Margret**
Gimme Love
RCA Victor, 1961

139 **Elvis Presley**
Blue Suede Shoes
RCA, 1984

140 **Bobby Darin**
Bullmoose
Atco, 1959

141 **Bobby Rydell**
I'll Never Dance Again
Cameo, 1962

142 **Jackie Gleason**
Music To Remember Her
Capitol, 1955

143 **Jerry Lee Lewis**
High School Confidential
Sun, 1958

144 **Skafish**
Disgracing The Family Name
Illegal, 1979

145 **Wazmo Nariz**
Tele-Tele-Telephone
Stiff, 1978

146 **Accident**
Kill The Bee Gees
No Threes, 1979

147 **The Accidents**
Blood Spattered With Guitars
Hook Line 'n' Sinker, 1979

148 **The Members**
Flying Again
Virgin, 1980
Designer: Malcm Garrat + Abiding Images

149 **Scud Mountain Boys**
Knievel+1
Sub Pop, 1995
Designer: Jeff Kleinsmith

150 **Joan Jett and the Blackhearts**
Spinster
Blackheart Records, 1994
Designer: Spencer Drate

151 **Ramones**
I Wanna Be Your Boyfriend
Norton, 1997
Photographer: Stephanie Chernikowski
Designer: Pete Ciccone

152 **The A-Bones**
Button Nose
Norton, 1991
Photographer: Stacy Zaferes
Designer: Pete Ciccone

153 **Dead Kennedys**
Too Drunk To Fuck
Cherry Red, 1981

154 **Yachts**
Box202
Radarscope, 1979

155 **The Clash**
London Calling
CBS, 1979

157 **Jessamine**
Your Head Is So Small It's Like A Little Light
Sup Pop, 1994

158 **Mudhoney**
Touch Me I'm Sick
Sub Pop, 1988
Photographer: Michael Lavine

The Murder City Devils/Gluecifer
In This Town
Sub Pop, 1999

160 **Sue Lyon**
Lolita Ya Ya
MGM, 1962

161 **The White Stripes**
Jolene
Third Man, 2004
Illustrator: Todd Slater
Designer: Rob Jones

162 **Murphy's Law**
Quality Of Life
Ng, 1998

163 **7 Year Bitch**
Men, Money And Moonshine
Mongoloid, 1992
Designer: Art Chantry

164 **Devo**
Mongoloid
Booji Boy, 1977
Photographer: Greg Kaiser
Designers: Jeff Seibert and Devo

165 **Death Wish Kids**
First Blood
Hopscotch, 2000
Designer: Brian Roettinger

166 **The Tremeloes**
Even The Bad Times Are Good
Epic, 1967

167 **The Zombies**
Tell Her No
Parrot, 1965

168 **The Mystery Girls**
EP
Strange, 1979

169 **Lambchop**
Nine
Merge, 1993

170 **Nirvana**
Sliver
Sub Pop, 1990
Photographer: Michael Lavine

171 **The Briefs**
C'mon Squash Me Like A Bug
Sub Pop, 2001

172 **Howlies**
Sea Level
OverUnder, 2008
Designers: N. DuPey, Stupid Tight Design

173 **Lulu**
To Sir With Love
Columbia, 1967

174 **Paul Simon**
You Can Call Me Al
Warner Brothers, 1986

175 **Pink Section**
Tour Of China
Pink Section, 1979

176 **Hugo Winterhalter and His Orchestra**
The Great Music Themes Of Television
RCA Victor, 1954

177 **The Moody Blues**
Your Wildest Dreams
PolyGram, 1986
Art Director: Alwyn Clayden
Illustrator: Kari Lloyd
Photographer: Michael Happen
Designers: Alwyn Clayden and Bruce Gill

178 Clockwise from top left:
U.S. Bonds
Quarter To Three
Legrand, 1961

Bobby Vinton
Long Lonely Nights
Epic, 1965

Jack Scott
Goodbye Baby
Carlton, 1958

Edd Byrnes
Kookie's Mad Pad
Warner Brothers, 1959

179 **Ritchie Valens**
Stay Beside Me
Del-Fi, 1959

180 **Cliff Richard and the Shadows**
Expresso Bongo
Columbia, 1960

181 **Esquerita**
Dew Drop Inn
Norton, 1992

182 **Helios Creed**
The Warming
Amphetamine Reptile, 1991
Designer: Haze

183 **Weirdos**
We Got The Neutron Bomb
Dangerhouse, 1978

184 **Thee Headcoats/Lollipop**
I Wanna Get Fucked
Amphetamine Reptile, 1997
Designer: Haze XXL

185 **Inger Lorre and Motel Shootout**
Burn
Sympathy for the Record Industry, 1994
Photographer: Kwaku Alston

186 **Sex Pistols**
Holidays In The Sun
Virgin, 1977

187 **The Beatles**
Free As A Bird
Apple, 1995
Illustrator: John Lennon
Designer: Richard Ward

188 **The Undertones**
Here Comes The Summer
Sire, 1979

189 **Eagles**
Please Come Home For Christmas
Asylum, 1978
Photographer: Michael Upright
Designers: Don Henley and Johnny Lee

190 **Raspberries**
Don't Want To Say Goodbye
Capitol, 1972

191 **Creedence Clearwater Revival**
Lookin' Out My Back Door
Fantasy, 1970

192 **Modest Mouse**
Broke
Sub Pop, 1996
Designer: Jeff Kleinsmith

193 **Simon and Garfunkel**
My Little Town
Columbia, 1975

194 **84 Flesh**
D-Section
Skydog, 1984

195 **Rats Into Robots**
Pretext For War
Magic Bullet, 2003
Photographer: Adam Lowe
Designer: Brent Eyestone

196 **Hollywood Brats**
Then He Kissed Me
Cherry Red, 1979

197 **Pretenders**
Talk Of The Town
Real, 1980

198 **Butterglory**
Our Heads
Merge, 1993

199 **Foo Fighters**
Learn To Fly
Roswell, 1999
Designer: P.R. Brown

200 **The Merseybeats**
On Stage
Fontana, 1964

201 **The Rolling Stones**
19th Nervous Breakdown
London, 1966

202 **Lockjaw**
Shock Value
Self Released, 1982

203 **The Billy Syndrome**
Karma
Slutfish Records, 1997
Photographer: André Grossmann
Art Director: Bill Ogilvie

204 **MX 80**
Someday You'll Be King
Ralph (Cryptic Corporation), 1980
Photographer: Kim Torgerson

205 **Steve Forbert**
Arriving Live
Nemperor, 1978
Photographer: David Gahr

206 **Grand Funk**
Walk Like A Man
Capitol, 1973

207 **Madness**
One Step Beyond...
Stiff, 1979

208 **The Blues Magoos**
There's A Chance We Can Make It
Mercury, 1967

209 **The Guess Who**
Laughing
RCA, 1969

210 **Laurie Anderson**
O Superman
One Ten, 1981
Graphics: Hoberman
Cover: Laurie Anderson

211 **The Searchers**
Another Night
Sire, 1981
Designer: Patrick Barber

212 **The Kinks**
Lola
BR Music, 1985

213 **Carpenters**
Rainy Days And Mondays
A&M, 1971

214 **Modo**
I Wish I Could Dance Like Fred Astaire
Deli Platters, 1980
Designer: Spencer Drate

215 **Plastic Bertrand**
Ça Plane Pour Moi
Sire, 1978
Designer: Spencer Drate

216 **Gary Lee Conner**
Grasshopper's Daydream
Sub Pop, 1999
Designer: Jeff Kleinsmith

217 **Social Distortion**
1945
13th Floor, 1981

218 **Frodus/Atomic Fireball**
Disco
Lovitt, 1999

219 **The Jam**
Absolute Beginners
Polydor, 1981

220 **Grand Funk**
We're An American Band
Capitol, 1973

221 **Navies**
House Ties
Lovitt, 2006
Photographer: Shayna Katherine Cohen
Designer: Anthony Decanini

222 **The Dictators**
I Am Right
Norton, 1996
Cover Art: Pete Ciccone
Photographer: Marieken Cochius

223 **The Rolling Stones**
We Were Falling In Love
Bootleg, 2003

224 **Jeff Beck**
Hi Ho Silver Lining
Columbia, 1967

225 **Elton John**
Mama Can't Buy You Love
MCA, 1979
Photographer: A3
Designer: Jubilee

226 **Stevie Wonder**
Fingertips, Part 1 & 2
Tamla, 1963

227 **The Turtles**
You Know What I Mean
White Whale, 1967

228 **Mickey and the Milkshakes**
Please Don't Tell My Baby
Milkshakes, 1982

229 Clockwise from top left:
The Easybeats
Friday On My Mind
United Artists, 1966

The Yardbirds
Still I'm Sad
Riviera, 1966

Flamin' Groovies
Slow Death
United Artists, 1972

Elton John and John Lennon
28th November 1974…
DJM, 1981
Photographer: Chuck Pulin

230 **The Rolling Stones**
It's All Over Now
London, 1964

231 **Four Tops**
Reach Out I'll Be There
Motown, 1966

232 **Gasoline**
I Just Low
Estrus, 1997
Designer: Art Chantry

233 **Ramones**
Don't Come Close
Sire, 1978
Designer: Spencer Drate

234 **Kate Bush**
Wuthering Heights
EMI, 1978

235 **Rick James**
This Magic Moment
Warner Brothers, 1989

236 **Jad Fair**
The Zombies Of Mora-Tau
Armageddon, 1982

237 **Mudhoney**
Night Of The Hunted
Super Electro Sound, 1998

238 **Antiseen**
We Got This Far (Without You)
Sub Pop, 1992
Photographer: Dee Clayton

239 **Avengers**
We Are The One
Dangerhouse, 1977
Photographer: Marcus Leatherdale

240 **The Pretenders**
My Baby
Sire, 1987

241 **Slayer and T.S.O.L**
Abolish Government
Sub Pop, 1996

243 **Killing Joke**
Wardance
Malicious Damage, 1980

244 **Joy Division**
Love Will Tear Us Apart
Factory, 1980

Minor Threat
In My Eyes
Dischord, 1981

246 **X—X (X Blank X)**
A
Drome Records, 1979
Photographer: J. Morton

247 **Ian Dury**
Sex & Drugs & Rock & Roll
Stiff, 1976

248 **Iggy and the Stooges**
Search And Destroy
Sundazed, 2005
Photographer: Mick Rock

249 **Joseph Arthur**
All Of Our Hands
14th Floor, 2004
Illustrator: Joseph Arthur

250 **The Makers**
Tiger Of The Night
Sub Pop, 2001
Photographer: Lance Hammond
Designer: Jesse LeDoux

251 **John Cale**
Ready For War
Spy, 1980
Designer: John Vogel

252 **Cave In**
Anchor
Magic Bullet, 2003
Photographer: Michael Lavine
Designer: Aaron Turner

253 **Minor Threat**
Minor Threat
Dischord, 1981
Photographer: Susie Josephson

254 **Multiple Artists**
Dope-Guns-'N-Fucking in the Streets (Volume Two)
Amphetamine Reptile, 1989
Designer: D. Deuteronomy

255 **The White Stripes**
Fell In Love With a Girl
XL, 2002

256 **Tom Petty and the Heartbreakers**
Listen To Her Heart
ABC, 1978

257 **The Kinks**
Waterloo Sunset
Flashbacks, 1967

258 Clockwise from top left:
Tommy James and the Shondells
I Think We're Alone Now
Roulette, 1967

The Animals
The House Of The Rising Sun
Rak, 1965

The Animals
I'm Crying
MGM, 1964

The Hollies
On A Carousel
Imperial, 1967

259 **The Rolling Stones**
Five By Five
Decca, 1964

260 **Plastic Ono Band**
Woman Is The Nigger Of The World
Apple, 1972

261 **Spooky Tooth**
Sunshine Help Me
Fontana, 1967

262 **Johnny Clash**
Old Clash Fan Fight Song
Johnny Clash, 2007

263 **Zen Guerrilla**
Dirty Mile
Estrus, 2001
Designer: Art Chantry

264 **Cardinal**
Toy Bell
Flydaddy, 1993
Designer: Jeff Kleinsmith

265 **Elliott Smith**
Pretty (Ugly Before)
Suicide Squeeze, 2003
Designer: Jesse LeDoux

266 **Blondie**
The Tide Is High
Chrysalis, 1980

267 **Vic Damone**
Engagement Party
Mercury, 1954

268 **Lene Lovich**
Angels
Stiff, 1980

269 **The Rolling Stones**
Saint Of Me
Virgin, 1998
Photographer: Maggie Steber
Designer: Jeff Lyons

270 **The Smiths**
Heaven Knows I'm Miserable Now
Rough Trade, 1984
Designer: Caryn Gough

271 **Dead Boys**
Sonic Reducer
Sire, 1977
Photographer: Glenn Brown

272 **The Cowsills**
The Rain, The Park & Other Things
MGM, 1967

273 **The Young Rascals**
Love Is A Beautiful Thing
Atlantic, 1966

274　**Richard Anthony**
La Leçon De Twist
Columbia, 1962

275　**Frank Sinatra**
A Swingin' Affair
Capitol, 1957

276　**Canned Heat**
Going Up The Country
Liberty, 1968

277　**The Onyas**
Live For Rejection
Man's Ruin, 1997

278–9　**Fun Lovin' Criminals**
King Of New York
Chrysalis, 1996
Photographer: Bob Gruen

280　**Guzzard**
Glued
Amphetamine Reptile, 1993
Photographer: Dan Corrigan
Designer: Haze

281　**XTC**
This Is Pop?
Virgin, 1978

282　**Be Your Own Pet**
Extra Extra
Dim Mak, 2006
Lettering: Jake Orrall
Illustrator: Nathan Vasquez
Designer: Nick Pimentel

283　**This Machine Kills/JR Ewing**
Take Back The Night
Wakusei, 2002

284　**The Zutons**
Pressure Point
Deltasonic, 2004

285　**The Zutons**
You Will You Won't…
Deltasonic, 2004

286　**Pigface**
Empathy
Sub Pop, 1993
Designer: Jeff Kleinsmith

287　**Cream**
Badge
RSO, 1982

288　**Q and Not U**
Hot And Informed
Dischord, 2000
Photographer: Shawn Brackbill

289　**Bob Beland**
Stealing Cars
Deli Platters, 1980
Photographer and designer: Mary Roth

290　**The Buckinghams**
Mercy, Mercy, Mercy
Columbia, 1967

291　Clockwise from top left:
The Spencer Davis Group
Time Seller
United Artists, 1967

The Yardbirds
Psycho Daisies
Epic, 1967

Nazz
Open My Eyes
ATCO, 1968

Pretenders
I Go To Sleep
Sire, 1981

292　**Speedy West and Jimmy Bryant**
2 Guitars Country Style
Capitol, 1954

293　**Elvis Presley**
The Real Elvis
RCA Victor, 1956

294　**The Boomtown Rats**
Rat Trap
Ensign, 1978
Photographer: Brian Aris

295　**Jacksons**
Body
Epic, 1984
Photographer: Mathew Rolston

296　**Arthur Lee**
Unissued 1965 Demos
Norton, 2006

297　**The Manish Boys & the Lower 3rd**
The Manish Boys
EMI, 1979

298　**David Bowie**
The Jean Genie
RCA, 1983

299　**Siouxsie & the Banshees**
Hong Kong Garden
Polydor, 1978
Designer: M. Nakamine

300　**Bum**
Debbiespeak
Lance Rock, 1991
Designer: Art Chantry

301　**Bananarama**
Shy Boy
London, 1982
Designers: Nick Egan and Pete Barrett

302 **Patty Smyth**
Downtown Train
Columbia, 1987
Photographer: Lynn Goldsmith

303 **T. Rex**
The Groover
Ariola, 1973

304 **Annette Funicello**
How Will I Know My Love?
Walt Disney, 1959

305 **The Honeycombs**
I Can't Stop
Interphon, 1964

306 Clockwise from top left:
Johnny Tillotson
Worry
MGM, 1964

Bobby Vee
How Many Tears
Liberty, 1961

Bobby Darin
That's The Way Love Is
ATCO, 1960

Dion
Ruby Baby
Columbia, 1963

307 **Sal Mineo**
Sal Sings
Epic, 1958

308 **Procol Harum**
A Whiter Shade Of Pale
Deram, 1967

309 **The Hullaballoos**
I'm Gonna Love You Too
Roulette, 1965

310 **The Chubbies**
I'm the King: The Demos
Sympathy for the Record Industry, 1995
Photographer: Matt Phuzz

311 **Bruce Springsteen**
Born In The U.S.A
Columbia, 1984
Photographer: Annie Leibovitz
Designer: Andrea Klein

312 **Bob Dylan**
Positively 4th Street
Columbia, 1965

313 **Elvis Presley**
You'll Think Of Me
RCA Victor, 1969

314 **Traffic**
Hole In My Shoe
Island, 1978
Designer: Michael Beal

315 **The Kinks**
Dandy
Pye, 1967

316 **Richard Hell & the Voidoids**
Blank Generation
Sire, 1977
Photographer: Roberta Bayley

317 **The Cramps**
Drug Train
Illegal, 1980
Photographer: Anton Corbijn
Designer: Vermilion Sands

318 **Flipper**
Love Canal
Subterranean, 1980

319 **The Piranhas**
I Don't Want My Body
Sire, 1980
Designer: J

320 **Shitbirds**
Oh Joy
Sympathy for the Record Industry, 1993
Illustrator: John Kricfalusi
Ink and Paint: Libby Simon

321 **The Rolling Stones**
Harlem Shuffle
Rolling Stones, 1986
Illustrator: Bakshi Productions

322 **The Left Banke**
Desirée
Smash, 1967

323 **The Bee Gees**
Spicks And Specks
Spin, 1966

324 **Herb Alpert & the Tijuana Brass**
Slick
A&M, 1968

325 **Trio**
Anna
Mercury, 1982

326 **Stealers Wheel**
Star
A&M, 1973

327 **Andy Gibb**
I Just Want To Be Your Everything
RSO, 1977

328 **Shirley Bassey**
Goldfinger
Columbia, 1981

329 **Mudhoney**
You Got It (Keep It Outta My Face)
Sub Pop, 1989
Photographer: Charles Peterson

331 **Dwarves**
She's Dead
Sub Pop, 1990

332 **Electric Eels**
Agitated
Rough Trade, 1978
Illustrator: John Morton

334 **Thee Headcoats**
When You Stop Lovin' Me
Sub Pop, 1993
Photographer: Kira
Designer: Jeff Kleinsmith

335 **Stymie**
Creepy Boss
New Rage, 1995

336 **Ugly Casanova**
Diggin' Holes
Sub Pop, 2002

337 **Forensics**
Boat Day At The Marina
Magic Bullet, 2003
Designer: Brent Eyestone

338 **The Hardship Post**
Watching You
Sub Pop, 1995
Designer: Hank Trotter

339 **Mission of Burma**
Academy Fight Song
Ace of Hearts Records, 1980
Designers: Steven Raffin and Margie Politzer

340 **Bread**
If
Elektra, 1970

341 **The Shadows of Knight**
Oh Yeah
Dunwich, 1966

342 **Country Joe and the Fish**
Thing Called Love
Rag Baby, 1966

343 **Steely Dan**
Rikki Don't Lose That Number
ABC, 1974

344 **The Everly Brothers**
Crying In The Rain
Warner Brothers, 1962

345 Clockwise from top left:
The Pretenders
Hymn To Her
Sire, 1986

Jackson Browne
Boulevard
Asylum, 1980

The Righteous Brothers
He Will Break Your Heart
Verve, 1966

Simon and Garfunkel
The Dangling Conversation
Columbia, 1966

346 **Frank & Moon Zappa**
Valley Girl
Barking Pumpkin, 1982

347 **Peaches & Herb**
Close Your Eyes
Date, 1967

348 **Multiple Artists**
All Star Rock And Roll
Atlantic, 1953

349 **Fatal Flying Guilloteens**
Shake Train
Estrus, 1999
Designer: Art Chantry

350 **Multiple Artists**
4 On The Floor
CZ, 1993
Designer: Art Chantry

351 **The Thrown Ups**
Eat My Dump
Amphetamine Reptile, 1988

352 **The Shaven**
Upsetting Mine
IMP/Rainforest, 1992

353 **Song of Zarathustra**
Poisonous Movement
Hand Held Heart, 2001

354 **Bert**
Spittle
Homo Habilis, 1994
Designer: Art Chantry

355 **Multiple Artists**
If I Were A Carpenter (disc 7 of 7)
A&M, 1994
Designer: Sunja Parc

356 **The Insomniacs**
Guilt Free!
Estrus, 1998

357 **Die Monitr Batss/A.S.T**
Untitled
Dim Mak, 2004

358 **Frank Kozik with Sonic Boom**
Loser
Sympathy for the Record Industry, 1994
Illustrator and designer: Kozik

359 **Tree**
Smash the State!
Man's Ruin, 1996

360 **Pogo the Clown**
Lederhosen
Amphetamine Reptile, 1988
Illustrators: M. Dancey and Haze

361 **Sylvester**
Someone Like You
Warner Brothers, 1986
Illustrator: Keith Haring

362 **JE + ILL/Joe Coleman**
Kiss & Kill
Sympathy for the Record Industry, 1993
Illustrator: Joe Coleman
Designer: Eddie Flowers

363 **The Wesley Willis Fiasco**
Split
Sympathy for the Record Industry, 1996

364 **Fleetwood Mac**
The Green Manalishi (With The Two Prong Crown)
Reprise, 1970

365 **Spooky Tooth**
Waitin' For The Wind
Island, 1969

366 **The Beach Boys**
Help Me, Rhonda
Capitol, 1965

367 **Dion and the Belmonts**
Where Or When
Laurie, 1959

368 **Paul Simon**
Mother And Child Reunion
Warner Brothers, 1988
Photographer: Robert Mapplethorpe

369 **Bruce Springsteen**
Hungry Heart
Columbia, 1980
Photographer: Joel Bernstein

370 **Truman's Water**
Miss Spaceship
Sub Pop, 2000

371 **Kelly Osbourne/Forensics**
Have Yourself A Merry Little Christmas
Sanctuary, 2005
Illustrator: Daniel Danger

372 **5ive Style**
Waiting On The Eclipse
Sub Pop, 1994
Illustrator: Chris Ware

373 **Andre Williams**
The Monkey Speaks His Mind!
Norton, 2002
Designer: Art Chantry

374 **The Beatles**
What Goes On
Capitol, 1966

375 **The Blues Project**
Where There's Smoke There's Fire!
Verve, 1966

376 **Rox**
American Kan Kan
EMI, 1987

377 **The Sweet**
Teenage Rampage
RCA Victor, 1974

378 **Band Aid**
Do They Know It's Christmas?
Columbia, 1984

379 Clockwise from top left:
Flat Duo Jets
I'll Have a Merry Christmas Without You
Norton, 1994
Illustrator: P. Bagge

Cricketones
Frosty The Snow Man
Cricket, 1953

The Untamed Youth
Santa's Gonna Shut 'Em Down
Norton, 1989
Illustrator: Chris Cooper

Ken Jay and the Cricketones
Rudolph The Red-Nosed Reindeer
Cricket, 1953

380 **Grace Jones**
Slave To The Rhythm
Island, 1985
Photographer: Jean-Paul Goude
Designers: Jean-Paul Goude and Greg Porto

381 **Nona Hendryx**
If Looks Could Kill (D.O.A.)
RCA, 1985

382 **Peggy Lipton**
Stoney End
Ode, 1968

383 **Melanie**
Ring The Living Bell
Neighborhood, 1972
Photographer: Maddy Miller
Designer: Bill Levy

384 **Superchunk**
The Majestic
Merge, 1999

385 **Live**
1999 Friends Of Live Holiday Gift Limited Edition
Action Front, 1999
Designer: Bruce Licher

386 **Creeper Lagoon**
The Fountain
Sub Pop, 1998
Designer: Jeff Kleinsmith

387 **Sow Belly**
Spaztech Culture
New Rage, 1991
Designer: Jeff Kleinsmith

388 **Impossible Five/The Jerks**
Split
Lovitt, 1996

389 Clockwise from top left:
Chixdiggit
Shadowy Bangers From A Shadowy Duplex
Sub Pop, 1996
Illustrator: Tom Bagley

Los Falanas
Tantrum
Sympathy for the Record Industry, 1993
Illustrator: Cooley High Pablo

Los Falanas
Hell Blues
Sympathy for the Record Industry, 1995
Illustrator: Pablo Tabasco

Chris Wilson
Sympathy For The Devil
Sympathy for the Record Industry, 1993
Illustrator: Pablo D'Ablo

390 **Servotron**
Meet Your Mechanical Masters
Sympathy for the Record Industry, 1995
Illustrator and designer: Shag

391 **Friends of Dean Martin**
Polena
Sub Pop, 1995
Designer: Hank Trotter

392 **Forensics**
The Green Lion
Timberline, 2007
Artwork: Brent

393 **Love 666**
XTC
Amphetamine Reptile, 1994
Illustrator and designer: Haze XXL

394 **Basil Wolverton**
Wolvertunes
Sympathy for the Record Industry, 1992

395 **The Dentists**
Charms And The Girl
Independent Project Records, 1992
Designer: Bruce Licher

396 **The Police**
Roxanne
A&M, 1978
Illustrator: Paul Allen
Designer: Michael Ross

397 **The Good Life**
Heartbroke
Saddle Creek, 2007
Artwork/layout: Zack Nipper
Hand-screened by: Joey Lynch

399 **Savage Republic**
Tragic Figure (2nd ed.)
Independent Project Records, 1984
Designer: Bruce Licher

400 **Savage Republic**
Tragic Figure (1st ed.)
Independent Project Records, 1984
Designer: Bruce Licher

Savage Republic
Film Noir (1st ed.)
Independent Project Records, 1983
Designer: Bruce Licher

401 **Savage Republic**
Film Noir (2nd ed.)
Independent Project Records, 1983
Designer: Bruce Licher

Savage Republic
Film Noir (3rd ed.)
Independent Project Records, 1983
Designer: Bruce Licher

402 **Indian Bingo/Ambulance**
IPR 10th Anniversary
Independent Project Records, 1990

403 Clockwise from top left:
Gene
Be My Light, Be My Guide [U.S.A.]
Sub Pop, 1995
Designer: Jeff Kleinsmith

Gene
Be My Light, Be My Guide [U.K.]
Sub Pop, 1995
Designer: Jeff Kleinsmith

S*M*A*S*H
Barrabas (Piloted)
Sub Pop, 1994
Designer: Jeff Kleinsmith

Supergrass
Lose It
Sub Pop, 1995
Designer: Jeff Kleinsmith

404 **Blowhole**
Staples
Apraxia, 1995

405 **Lord High Fixers/Gasoline**
Young Man Blues
Estrus, 1998
Designers: Art Chantry and Dave Crider

406 **Indian Bingo**
Big Rock
Independent Project Records, 1991

407 **The Residents**
Satisfaction
Ralph (Cryptic Corporation), 1976

408 **Discharge**
Fight Back
Clay, 1980

409 **Alberto Y Lost Trios Paranoias**
Snuff Rock
Stiff, 1977

410 **3Ds**
Beautiful Things
Merge, 1993

411 **Multiple Artists**
Buy Or Die!
Ralph (Cryptic Corporation), 1980
Illustrator: Gary Panter

412 **Whopping Big Naughty**
Your Not Coming
Amphetamine Reptile, 1993

413 **Worst Case Scenario**
Studies In Pessimism
Lookout, 1995

414 **Jale**
All Ready
Sub Pop, 1996
Designer: Jeff Kleinsmith

415 **R.E.M.**
Baby Baby
R.E.M., 1991
Designer: Bruce Licher

416 **The Diplomats of Solid Sound**
Pork Chop
Estrus, 2002
Designers: Art Chantry and Dave Crider

417 **Stymie**
Other
New Rage, 1993
Designer: Jeff Kleinsmith

418 **Ism**
I Think I Love You
S.I.N., 1983
Designer: Jism/Sallese

419 **Steppenwolf**
Born To Be Wild
Capitol, 1971

420 **The Doll**
Desire Me
Beggar's Banquet, 1979
Photographer: Bob Carlos Clarke

421 **Cherry Red**
Get Set
Feralette, 1995
Photographer: Spencer Lloyd
Designer: Judy Hudson

422 **Peter Frampton**
I'm In You
A&M, 1977

423 **Trini Lopez**
Sad Tomorrows
Reprise, 1964

424 **John Lennon/Yoko Ono**
Nobody Told Me
Polydor, 1984

425 **John Lennon**
Every Man Has A Woman Who Loves Him
Polydor, 1984
Photographer: Bob Gruen

426 **Dread Zeppelin**
Your Time Is Gonna Come
I.R.S., 1990
Designer: Fred Zeppelin

427 **New Wave Hookers**
Crystal Bullet
Estrus, 1998
Designer: Art Chantry

428 **Michael Jackson**
The Way You Make Me Feel
Epic, 1987
Photographer: Sam Emerson

429 **Barbra Streisand**
Love theme from *A Star Is Born (Evergreen)*
Columbia, 1976

430 **Joan Jett and the Blackhearts**
I Love You Love
Blackheart Records, 1984
Photographer: Brian Aris
Designers: Spencer Drate and Judith Salavetz

431 **Fleetwood Mac**
Gypsy
Warner Brothers, 1982

432 **Paradise Island**
Deprogram Getup
Dim Mak, 2003

433 **Vampire Weekend**
Mansard Roof
Abeano, 2007
Photographer: Alexis Boling

434 Clockwise from top left:
This Machine Kills
On The Move
El Grito, 2000

Talk Talk
Life's What You Make It
EMI, 1986
Illustrator: James Marsh

Butterfly Train
Blame Weight
Up, 1994
Designer: Hank Trotter

Halo of Flies
No Time
Amphetamine Reptile, 1988
Designer: Haze XXL

435 **Halo of Flies**
F.T.W.
Amphetamine Reptile, 2007
Designer: Haze XXL

436 **Plexi**
Part Of Me
Sub Pop, 1995
Designer: Jeff Kleinsmith

437 **Quadrajets**
Bad Mojo At The Border
Sub Pop, 2000
Photographer: Lance Hammond
Designer: Jeff Kleinsmith

438 **Ian Dury and the Blockheads**
Hit Me With Your Rhythm Stick
Stiff, 1978

439 **Steel Wool**
Broom Sauce
Empty, 1992
Illustrator: Ian Hallam
Designer: STD

440 **Oiler**
Scarif
Sympathy for the Record Company, 1993
Illustrator: Justin Forbes

441 **Thee HeadcoaTees**
We Got 7 Inches But We Wanted Twelve!
Sympathy for the Record Industry, 1991
Illustrator: Alan Forbes

442 **Rocket from the Crypt**
On the Prowl
Sympathy for the Record Industry, 2003
Illustrator and designer: Nathan Cabrera

443 Clockwise from top left:
Electric Frankenstein
The Perfect Crime
Sub Pop, 2000
Illustrator: Vidor

The Hellacopters
Down Right Blue
Sub Pop, 1999
Illustrator: Peter Bagge
Designer: Jeff Kleinsmith

Satan's Cheerleaders
Roller Coaster
Sympathy for the Record Industry, 1994
Illustrator: Chris Cooper

The Mummies/The Wolfmen
The Mummies VS The Wolfmen
Sympathy for the Record Industry, 1991
Illustrator: Chris Cooper

444 **Electric Eels**
Agitated
Rough Trade, 1978
Illustrator: John Morton

445 **The Smithereens**
Girls About Town
D-Tone, 1980
Illustrator: Justine Strait

446 **Brenda Lee**
My Whole World Is Falling Down
Decca, 1963

447 **Connie Francis**
Second Hand Love
MGM, 1962

448 **The Pointed Sticks**
I'm Numb
Quintessence, 1979

449 **Supergrass**
Kiss Of Life
Parlophone, 2004

450 **The Adverts**
One Chord Wonder
Stiff, 1977

451 **Scarling**
Band Aid Covers The Bullet Hole
Sympathy for the Record Industry, 2003
Illustrator: Mark Ryden

452 **Richard Hell**
Another World
Ork, 1976
Photographer: Roberta Bayley

453 **The Rolling Stones**
Cocksucker Blues
Hard-On, 1976

454 **Bryan Adams**
The Only Thing That Looks Good On Me Is You
A&M, 1996
Designer: Dirk Rudolph

455 **Dech Dans Face**
Merry Dickmass
Sub Pop, 1996
Photographers: Miss Nathalia and Mr. DID

456 **Aughra**
Habidabad Vol. 1
Underadar, 2004
Designer: Brent Eyestone

457 **The Anniversary**
What's My Name? My Name Is What?
Sub Pop, 2001

458 **Spongegod**
Mimi Rogers
Coolidge Records, 1993

459 **The Jars**
Time Of The Assassins
Universal, 1980

460 **David Bowie**
Sorrow
RCA Victor, 1973

480 **The Makers**
Music to Suffer By
Estrus Records, 1995

ABOUT THE CONTRIBUTORS

ERIC DAVIDSON
For thirteen years, Eric Davidson was the yalper in the Columbus, Ohio, punk band New Bomb Turks, and has been a freelance writer for even longer. He was recently the associate editor at *CMJ* for a goodly spell, and is currently finishing his first book about '90s garage punk.

JOHN FOSTER
The principal and superintendent of the design firm Bad People Good Things LLC, John Foster is a world-renowned designer, author, and speaker. He is the author of *Dirty Fingernails: A One-of-a-Kind Collection of Uniquely Designed Graphics by Hand*, *For Sale: Over 200 Innovative Solutions in Packaging Design*, *New Masters of Poster Design*, and *Maximum Page Design*, as well as a forthcoming monograph on the work of Jeff Kleinsmith for Sub Pop Records. His work has appeared in publications and galleries all over the world, including the permanent collection of the Smithsonian Institute.

STUART GOLDMAN
Stuart Goldman is a documentary producer based in New York and Los Angeles. His films include *Elvis in Hollywood*, about Elvis' legendary movies of the 1950s; *Elvis and June*, the story of the singer's first fiancée in 1956; and *Alberta Hunter: My Castle's Rockin'*, a music biography of the blues singer/songwriter; among others. An avid collector in his teenage years, Goldman has more 45s than he knows what to do with.

TOM HAZELMYER
After cutting his teeth on the late-'70s and early-'80s Minneapolis punk/hardcore scene, Tom Hazelmyer (a.k.a. Haze XXL) spun his garage-band roots into Halo of Flies, became a darling of the underground press, and founded the proto-indie label Amphetamine Reptile Records, which has been noted for its roster of noise-rock artists and innovative record sleeve designs. All while honing his graphic chops with everything from flyers at the inception of hardcore to album covers and posters for the underground music scene throughout the '80s and '90s, Hazelmyer's years with AmRep led to his heavy involvement with the then-fledgling Lowbrow/Juxtapoz art movement. Starting in the late '90s, he hosted many of those same artists through OX-OP Arts Gallery and Projects. On days he's not busy trying to figure out why the second mouse gets the cheese, Haze can be found drinking at Grumpy's Bar in Minneapolis.

LENNY KAYE
A musician, writer, and record producer, Lenny Kaye has been a guitarist for poet-rocker Patti Smith since her band's inception more than thirty years ago. He is the coauthor of *Waylon*, Waylon Jennings' life story, and the author of *You Call It Madness: The Sensuous Song of the Croon*, a study of the romantic singers of the 1930s. In addition to his solo projects, he has worked in the studio with artists such as Suzanne Vega, Soul Asylum, Jim Carroll, and Allen Ginsberg. His seminal anthology of '60s garage-rock, *Nuggets*, has long been regarded as defining a genre.

BRUCE LICHER
Musician, artist, graphic designer, and letterpress printer, Bruce Licher is the founder of Independent Project Records & Press and Licher Art & Design. In early 1982, Licher learned the art of letterpress printing to create album covers for his band, Savage Republic, and shortly thereafter started designing and printing album covers for his record label, as well as for other groups and labels. A two-time Grammy nominee for his album packaging, Licher is generally credited with starting the trend in letterpress-printed CD and record packaging using industrial-style chipboard. His work has been featured in major design exhibitions at the Cooper-Hewitt National Design Museum in New York City. Licher currently lives and works in Sedona, Arizona.

ACKNOWLEDGMENTS

The authors would like to express their heartfelt appreciation to Elizabeth Sullivan, Dinah Fried, and Iris Shih, who recognized the vision and meaning of this special book. Great thanks also to the writers who captured the unique energy of the 45 sleeves so well: Lenny Kaye, Bruce Licher, Tom Hazelmyer, Stuart Goldman, Eric Davidson, and John Foster. Without generous cooperation and support from collectors, this book would never have been possible, so thank you Stuart Goldman, Bruce Alexander, Lenny Kaye, Adam Wahler, Hugh Brown, Justin Frohwirth, Larry Jaffee, Mark Arm, Steve Turner, Bob Gruen, and many contributing record labels. Finally, we offer a special salute to Brendan Dalton, who dove lovingly into the graphics with us, contributing mightily, and to our patient supporters and most honest critics, Ned Davis and Justin Kavoussi.

MUSIC TO SUFFER BY

The Makers

It's Your World
Baby Let Me Take You Home
She Should Be Cryin'